Psychology and the Superior Athlete

Psychology and the

Superior Athlete

MIROSLAV VANEK   CHARLES UNIVERSITY, PRAGUE, CZECHOSLOVAKIA

BRYANT J. CRATTY   UNIVERSITY OF CALIFORNIA, LOS ANGELES

The Macmillan Company / Collier-Macmillan Limited, London

FOREWORD

by J. E. Kane

The increasing interest in the psychological aspects of athletic performance probably reflects both the search by athletes, teachers, and coaches for the more elusive nonphysical determinants of success and the discovery by psychologists that the athletics arena is a fruitful laboratory for behavioral research. It would be naive to think, however, that psychological insights into the motivation and performance of the athlete have had to wait for modern methods of research and evaluation. Outstanding coaches have always used psychological principles in an intuitive way and the Olympic archives contain detailed psychological data and observation of athletes that were collected by de Coubertin and others. Nevertheless it has had to wait for the establishment of the International Society for Sports Psychology in 1965 for the organised exchange of information and opinion between serious researchers in sports psychology throughout the world. Already there is evidence that their common interest in sport has brought together psychologists from widely separated parts of the world and different 'schools' of psychology, and that the resulting collaboration has been fruitful and rewarding.

Not only does this text by Miroslav Vanek and Bryant Cratty clearly represent the value of international cooperation but it must also increase the guilt reaction of many English-speaking sports psychologists at their shameful ignorance of developments and researches in psychology that are proceeding in continental Europe. The happy arrangement which has made it possible for Vanek and Cratty to work together has enabled us all to benefit by virtue of the bridging of the East-West gap, and it has allowed these authors to represent the special values of experimental and clinical procedures of research in sports psychology.

We may now be entering the stage in this area of psychology of proposing certain theoretical constructs and models to explain the variation in performance of the superior athlete. Although they correctly hedge their speculations with appropriate reservation, Vanek and Cratty have given us, for the first time, a number of lines of approach towards a theory of sports performance based on a wider source of empiric evidence than has so far been drawn together. The sections dealing with motives, field studies, and a suggested typology of athletic activities seem to me to be particularly helpful in this respect in that ideas and evidence are presented from which hypotheses may be formulated and tested. Moreover, there are a number of highly interesting but small-scale researches outlined in the text that invite replication and expansion, and for this reason I am sure that some researchers will find here a valuable source of inspiration. The authors are to be highly commended both for their synthesis of material and for the stimulation their text will undoubtedly give to further work in sports psychology.

J. E. K.

PREFACE

I first met Dr. Miroslav Vanek in Rome in 1967 while we were both
attending the Fifth International Psychosomatic Medicine Week and
were presenting papers on the day devoted to the psychosomatics of
sport. Our viewpoints on research, sports, and physical activity seemed
to coincide at our initial meeting with each other, and he invited me to
visit Czechoslovakia and other countries in Eastern Europe the following
week. Although I had to refuse his kind invitation because of pressing
business in the United States, I invited him to visit my laboratory at the
University of California, Los Angeles, following the Mexican Olympics.

Following the 1968 Olympics we again worked together at the Second
International Congress of Sports Psychology in Washington, D.C., for
a week, and then spent three months together in Los Angeles. I became
aware of Dr. Vanek's impressive academic credentials and his vast knowledge of the psychology of sport during the first weeks we lived together.
I found that he had just been appointed to the chair of Sports Psychology
at Charles University earlier that year, and that he was working on his
third doctor's degree! I discovered that not only was he the author of
three books, but that his articles had been translated into several lan-
guages, including Japanese. His knowledge of experimental literature
dealing with motor activity and the psychology of sports seemed in-
exhaustible. His ability to speak Russian, French, German, and English,
together with the ability to read Italian, Spanish, and Polish, was mind-
boggling to a former language "student" who was nearly asked to leave
the university after several unsuccessful confrontations with freshman
French.

More than that, Dr. Vanek proved to be a charming guest who was kind and gracious to all those he met while in the United States. They, in turn, returned his kindness, and thus it became further apparent that his success with athletes and his being appointed the team psychologist to the Czechoslovakian Olympic Team was due to more than just his scholarly attainments.

After a couple of restless weeks with me it was obvious that Vanek wanted to get to work on something. Attempting to be a good host, I suggested that "sometime we should do an article about sports psychology—'Preparation of the Superior Athlete,' or some similar topic." He would not be put off, and next evening we embarked upon the "article" that an hour later took on the proportions of a chapter and that by the end of the week began to assume the guise of a full-length book.

The ideas he talked about, I knew, would be entirely new to American readers. And while at times the research described was not the well-polished statistical effort seen often in American psychological journals, the ingenuity which the studies reflected revealed entire areas of investigation which had apparently escaped scholars interested in physical activity in the United States.

Our initial evening stretched to three weeks of concentrated effort. Materials were needed in boxes that had been shipped from Mexico City and had mysteriously failed to arrive, but at the end of a month a rough two hundred and fifty pages of typed manuscript had appeared, which then was polished in the time remaining.

He was fascinated by much of what he encountered in America. He became an instant U.C.L.A. football and basketball fan, admiring not only the vigor of the games but the color associated with it, including the band, the "cheer girls," and the enthusiastic rooters.

But in a way the book was therapy, for after five months away from Prague, Miroslav missed his homeland, his family, his students, and his work at Charles University.

During our time together, I became fascinated with the man, with his ideas, and with the context in which the research on and preparation of the superior athlete had apparently flourished. I have tried to transmit some of what I heard from Miroslav Vanek to you, the reader. I hope, however, that between the lines you might discern some of Miroslav's basic philosophy. He seemed to be telling me that one must be scholarly and practical; sensitive and still aware and decisive; and that one should not become preoccupied only with numbers on research reports, but should also attempt to learn about people.

Dr. Vanek and I are both grateful to four people who worked very hard to help us prepare the manuscript. Mrs. Anna Carillo, Miss Sara Dobbins, and Mr. Jeff Drucker aided in the final typing and editorial work, and performed with diligence and expertise. Miss Berthe Vandervelde drew our illustrations with style and originality. We also would like to thank her for her excellent job. We are both grateful to Dr. Vaclav Hocek, C.Sc., whose collaboration with Dr. Vanek resulted in data upon which some of the material in the text is based.

B. J. C.

CONTENTS

1

OVERVIEW OF
PSYCHOLOGY AND THE
SUPERIOR ATHLETE

Dᴜʀɪɴɢ ᴛʜᴇ past fifty years numerous behavioral scientists in Europe have focused attention upon the psyche of the superior athlete. Their findings were given particular heed by coaches in the Eastern European countries after the 1960 Melbourne Olympics as they began to perceive the importance of sound psychological evaluation and training of athletes. At times this interest coalesced into reasonable objective laboratory experiments exploring the capacities of the elite sports performer, at other times field tests were contrived, while still a third approach was to analyze behavior of individuals and groups of sports performers within the actual game situations.

These data have contributed in several ways to a better understanding of human behavior. Some of the findings have, of course, resulted in better management of athletic endeavors in which country is pitted against country. Other observations have been helpful in exploring the manner in which physical education may result in the improvement of the normal child, while a third outcome of this research has been to formulate principles pertinent to the understanding of behavior under stress.

At times this type of "psychologizing" has taken the form of philosophical and moral statements that have only vague meanings. However, at other times the experiments and the subsequent outcomes have resulted in important lessons for English-speaking coaches and teachers of physical education.

In any case, the vast bulk of data, theorizing, and the formulation of helpful psychological training techniques

3

have not been available in English. It is the purpose of this text to attempt to summarize some of this information.

The material which follows is organized into several sections. The initial one deals with the history of sport psychology. Covered specifically are the beginnings of this subdiscipline which occurred shortly after the Russian revolution and blossomed in the 1920's. This initial section is followed by chapters in which the research methodologies are described, including experiments in the laboratory as well as those in the field. The next section contains information arising from experiments with superior sportsmen and sportswomen. The final section presents a discussion of how these findings have been utilized to improve the performance of top athletes in national and international competition. General operating principles are covered as well as the manner in which specific athletes (who will go unnamed) have been exposed to the techniques described.

It has been attempted to present the material that follows in language that is relatively simple. At times the information contained in the chapters is based upon research data, and when this is the case, the investigations have been cited. In many cases, however, the content is based upon personal experiences of the authors. It is hoped that the latter approach will inspire further research which will invalidate or substantiate some of the authors' speculations and inferences.

In the final chapter, material contained in the text has been summarized. In addition this section contains a review of some of the areas of knowledge which might be explored with further research.

It is believed that superior athletic performance has benefited from knowledge about the physiology and biomechanics of human motor activity. The authors, together with many coaches and psychologists throughout the world, however, believe that future records will be broken primarily because of increased attention to the psychological parameters of the human personality. For example,

Ozolin, the Russian track-and-field coach, has stated that future improvements in performance will come about through attention to the psychological training of athletes.

Many English-speaking coaches may be skeptical about attempts to scientifically "psych up" (or out) their athletes. They may claim that winning depends upon hard training methods and the availability of superior facilities rather than upon close attention to the emotional climate of the training camp or to the personality characteristics of their athletes. The number of medals won by American athletes in particular in the Olympics would seem to add weight to their words.

At the same time, however, it may be true that American athletes win in international competition in spite of insensitive coaches. They have excelled and probably will continue to evidence superior performance because of the large number of participants, the superior training facilities, as well as the diet to which they are exposed since childhood.

The writers are of the belief, however, that even more superlative performances will be evidenced if some of the principles and techniques outlined on the pages that follow are adhered to. It is believed thus that careful consideration of this material may make an important contribution to our knowledge about human performance in a broad sense as well as about vigorous activity on the athletic field and in the gymnasium.

CHAPTER 1

A Brief History of Sport Psychology

The Beginnings

In both Europe and the United States the studies and interest in motor ability and motor learning, during the past thirty-five years, have contributed in indirect ways to the understanding of superior athletes. In the United States relatively few studies and even fewer scholars focused upon superior athletes directly. In Europe, however, particularly in the countries of Eastern Europe, more concentrated efforts were made during this period of time to understand the psychological problems of athletes engaging in international competitions. In Europe and in the United States it is often difficult to separate the development of psychology from the evolution of sport psychology and indeed it is helpful if we consider the two inseparable, especially when studying the earlier periods of development.

The early philosophers speculated about motor function and perceptual awareness of movement. In the writings of Plato, Aristotle, and others it is possible to find references to important mind-body relationships that later were to become the subjects for psychological experimentation. The great minds of ancient Greece suggested that education should pay equal heed to the development of the mind and the body. (111)

The statues of the early years reflected this mind-body balance and depicted clever faces with determined gazes atop well-developed bodies. By the close of the Golden Era, however, the emphasis began to be

7

placed upon winning athletic contests. Professional boxers were trained in the larger cities; statues became more heavily muscled and their faces did not reflect the same intentness that was formerly seen. Some of the problems seen in connection with superior athletes and international competition in the nineteenth century had their roots in ancient Greece.

During the Middle Ages the human body was scorned by the theologians. No sport activity was permitted in connection with educational and cultural events. Only activities that in some way contributed to military excellence were prevalent, i.e., riding, fencing, archery, javelin throwing, and the like.

In opposition to theological separatism, which scorned the body in deference to the spiritual uplifting that was prevalent during the Dark Ages, the Renaissance spread its light over Europe and enlightened humanists incorporated physical activity into educational programs in France, Switzerland, Germany, and later in England. Hackensmith has described this period of transition in his 1966 text. (38)

Comenius, in Czechoslovakia, for example, divided the ideal day for the child into three equal parts: one to be devoted to sleep, the second to intellectual development, and the third to physical recreation of various kinds. Comenius suggested that as the human soul is nourished through books, so must the body be nourished through movement. (19) John Locke, an eighteenth-century Englishman, also developed an educational system in which sports and games played a major role. (111)

Guts Muths of Germany similarly laid some of the philosophical foundations for sport psychology. He stated that a child's play was his preparation for life, and furthermore that educators should attempt to devise programs which would aid children to find a balance in life between work and play. (111)

Pestalozzi, a Swiss, also suggested that exercise contributed in a positive way to what today would be termed "sound emotional adjustment" or "mental hygiene." He further suggested that physical exercise could hasten the total intellectual development of normal children and could also aid remediation of mental retardation in atypical children. (111)

The Czechoslovakian philosopher Tyrs, who was an exercise devotee himself, attempted in the middle 1800's to relate Darwin's emerging theories to physical exercise. He explained that those inclined to participate and excel in physical activities were those who through selection would also strive and achieve in other areas of competence and thus were the forerunners of generations of even more superior offspring. (48)

Thus the roots of sport psychology may be traced from many sources. Early contributions to thought in this area include statements and practices from ancient Greece, from Renaissance Europe, and from pedagogists from the late 1700's and early and middle 1800's. While many concentrated upon the physical and physiological changes well known to those participating in motor activities, a separate philosophical interest appeared very early which implied that sports activity involves more than muscles, bones, and breath.

The Roots of Experimental Psychology—1880–1920

Psychology as a science first appeared in the laboratory established at Leipzig by Wilhelm Wundt. (109) Prior to this the roots of psychology had begun to sprout in philosophy, medicine, and education. Wundt and his students were interested in perception and sensation and proposed that human mentality could be divided into three components—cognition, emotion, and volition (will power). In connection with these early studies of perception the psychologists of Central Europe were also concerned with motor learning, motor responses, motor-intellectual relationships, and the like.

The early experiments in sensation that led to psychophysical laws were derived from investigations in which kinesthetic perceptions of the differences in hand-held weights were measured.

Before the turn of the century, experiments were carried out in kinesthesis and various facets of sports performance both in Europe and the United States. In 1898 Triplett studied what he termed "dynamogenic factors" (the audience effect) upon bicycle-riding endurance. (92) In the same year Bowditch and Southard attempted to determine the comparative accuracy of vision versus kinesthetic judgments. (10) A year later Woodworth, in the United States, published a classic investigation in which various basic aspects of kinesthetics were measured. (108)

Behaviorists in Europe and the United States similarly formulated theoretical frameworks in which motor responses of animals and men played an important part. Pavlov and his students in his "Tower of Silence" studied conditioned reflexes in dogs, monkeys, and children. (69) Thorndike, in the United States, began to study motivation and at times employed handwriting tasks in his experiments with school children. (100)

Watson explored learning by observing the chaining together of motor responses of rats in mazes. (104) Allport, Skinner, Yerkes, and others at Harvard began to formulate the important theoretical bases of operant conditioning, personality theory, and animal behavior. (1), (91), (110)

Thus by the end of the second decade of the nineteenth century a number of theoretical and experimental threads may be discerned which later contributed to the beginnings of sport psychology in the fields of physical education and psychology. A scientific awakening seemed imminent in physical education. Physical educators seemed to be attempting to expand their understanding of physical activity. They seemed to be looking beyond the statements of the physicians who first supported their programs in the United States, and suggesting that perhaps emotional, social, and personality change could be elicited by exercise and game participation. At the same time, experimental psychology, although at times dissipating its energy in the struggle between systems and theories, had begun to establish a pool of basic knowledge about motor responses, motor learning, and the perception of movement.

During the 1890's and the early 1900's a number of trends may be discerned which later contributed to the emergence of sport psychology after World War I. For example, in 1896 Karl Groos wrote the *Play of Animals* and three years later wrote *Human Play*, suggesting that play, both for animals and humans, constituted a training ground for later life. (36)

In later years a number of authors similarly incorporated play into various psychological theories. Freud, for example, suggested that while play has some sexual overtones, it is also useful in emancipating the human ego, as the former may quickly take the form of passivity or activity in childhood. (27) Buehler in 1918 wrote about the pleasure of bodily activity received through play. (12) Buytendijk in 1933 also formulated a theory of play having psychological ramifications. (13) Buytendijk attributed many functions to play, including the following: preparing for life, reduction of excess energy, self-realization, and also at times providing a therapeutic release of unhealthy tensions and aggressions.

The psychological parameters of play had been commented upon by some authors. Motor activity and kinesthetics had been studied in several experimental laboratories in Germany and in America. Activation, motivation, and arousal had been explored by others.

Thus by the turn of the century a number of trends had appeared in what was formerly classified as "general psychology." These trends later coalesced into what would be termed "sport psychology" following World War I in Europe. The beginnings of social psychology were discernible in the writings of some Europeans and Americans.

Motor Learning, Sport Psychology, and Motor Behavior in Germany, 1900–1939

According to Antonelli, in his text titled *The Psychology and Psychopathology of Sport*, texts concerning the psychology of soccer appeared as early as 1801 in Europe (by Strutt). (2) One hundred years later (1901), a text by Jusserand also appeared in which various psychological parameters of soccer were discussed. In 1903 a similar text authored by Patrick appeared.

De Coubertin in Paris wrote a text titled *Essays in Sport Psychology*, in which sports were explored as a means of aesthetic expression, as a tool of education, and as a way to attain better emotional balance. (22) In 1912 in Germany a book by Barth on the influence of physical activity upon will power and character appeared. (6) The book explored ways in which physical exercise might contribute to the character development of sport participants. These texts, while using the term *psychology*, were, by and large, philosophical essays rather than scientific treatments of the subject.

World War I and Afterward

Following World War I several institutes in Europe initiated courses dealing with the training of physical educators in the psychology of sport and of physical activity. For example, a team of three psychologists in the Institute of Physical Education in Leipzig and Berlin started this type of curriculum offering.

From 1921 to 1928, R. W. Schulte, N. Sippel, and F. Giese all wrote textbooks on the psychology of physical activity. Their titles reflected the manner in which psychological parameters of physical activity were beginning to receive closer attention by European physical educators.

The topics of their texts covered a wide range of philosophical, experimental, and practical approaches possible in the psychology of physical activity. A text in 1921 by Schulte, for example, was titled *Body and Soul in Sport* and was primarily a philosophical work attempting to relate mind-body concepts. (85) A second work by Schulte, which was called *Ability and Performance Testing in Sport,* presented a battery of physical ability tests which might be employed in evaluating the physical proficiency of children in school. (86) A third work in 1924 was the first book to deal with the psychological preparation of superior athletes and was called *Increasing Performance in Exercises, Games and Sport Activities.* (87) In this latter text Schulte writes of the manner in which the coach could accommodate to individual differences in athletes' personality and ability trait structures. Teamwork, group interaction, pre-start tensions, and similar topics are also discussed by Schulte in this classic text.

About 1920 Sippel investigated the effects of various types of physical education programs upon measures of classroom performance. Tests of memory, concentration, and similar measures were given to children before and after programs of physical activity that varied in intensity. He found there was an optimum amount of physical stress that was likely to result in a maximum amount of classroom success. Too hard a program of physical activity or too passive a program did not prove as effective as one of a moderate degree of intensity. These studies were published in two books, *Physical Education in Schools and the Mental Work of School Children* and *Physical Exercises and Mental Activity.* (89), (90)

The third member of the research team at Leipzig, Giese, was also active as an author. In addition to two texts with a philosophical emphasis—*Soul of the Body* (1924) and *Spirit in Sport* (1925)—a booklet titled *Psychotechniques in Physical Education* (1928) outlined a number of performance tests which could be administered in order to assess the physical competencies of school children. (34), (32), (33)

At the University of Leipzig, just prior to World War II, Otto Klemm wrote several texts, including *Ideas About Physical Education* (1931) and *Twelve Principles in the Psychology of Physical Exercise* (1938). (44), (45) Klemm's first text dealt with the influence of exercise upon educational attainment, and it attempted to differentiate in academic attainment between schools that did and those that did not have physical education programs. The second book represented one of the first texts dealing with motor learning, motor ability, and transfer of skill. Various perceptual-motor relationships were discussed within a framework provided by Gestalt learning theory. In this latter text the results of ten years of experimentation (1928–1938) were utilized as the basis for the principles he derived. Krueger and Klemm in 1938 wrote a text titled *Motorics* that is one of the first modern books dealing with motor learning. (49)

Following World War II

In 1950, following World War II, the Institute of Physical Culture (Deutsche Hochschule fur Koerperkultur) was reorganized in Leipzig and continued to function as a training and research institute. The Institute was organized into two primary sections. One was a Research Institute of Physical Culture in which a Laboratory of Sport Psychology was established, and the second was termed the Training School for Physical Educators, in which a new chair of Sports Psychology was established. Dr. Paul Kunath was the first to occupy it. Kunath's staff in the Institute was influenced to a marked degree by similar staffs in Moscow and Leningrad. Exchange students and professors frequently traveled between the Russian institutions and the one in Leipzig to study and to lecture.

Among the topics they studied at Leipzig was motor learning, particularly studies based upon physiological psychology established by Pavlov. During the 1950's and early 1960's the superior athlete was similarly accorded attention in their investigations. Telemetric apparatus was employed in order to explore relationships between performance activation and the physical readiness to perform. Long-term observational techniques were used to study the superior athlete because the researchers were generally skeptical of the validity of tests of personality traits and of intelligence.

In 1966 and 1967 psychologists accompanied the German teams to high-altitude training sites in Bulgaria, as well as to pre-Olympic training in Mexico. Individuals taking a prominent role in this pre-Olympic training were Renate Mathesius and Sigmund Mueller, both of whom worked with Kunath at the University of Leipzig.

During this period of time, Mathesius and Mueller utilized self-rating scales on which athletes reported their feelings, as well as rating scales on athletes that were filled out by coaches. In addition to these more subjective measures, the German Olympians, after being subjected to the natural high-altitude stresses of Mexico City and Bulgaria, as well as being exposed to high-altitude chambers at the University of Leipzig, were given various tests of psychomotor performance, concentration, and mental ability. The German team psychologists avoided personality scales and projective tests. Neither did they attend the final Olympics in 1968, as they perceived their roles as scientists supportive to the German coaches, not as clinicians applying their findings and backgrounds directly to the athletes themselves.

Every three years, staff members alternate between teaching and researching. At the present time in Leipzig, a staff of about twelve graduate students and staff members is working on a number of research projects. The studies are dealing with motor learning, the influence of physical education upon character and the intellect, aspiration level, motivation, and investigations of attitudes toward physical activity.

S. Mueller published in the 1961 edition of *Bulletin of Theory and Practice of Physical Culture,* "Success and Failure in Sports as a Psychological Problem," and a study of "Pre-Start Tensions in Boxers." (58), (59) In 1963 Professor Kunath wrote *Psychology, Introduction for Extramural Studies* (50), a textbook for the students at Leipzig. In 1960 an important book dealing with motor learning was written by Kurt Meinel titled *Bewegungslehre.* (56) The book contains theoretical approaches from Leipzig to motor development, motor learning, and the acquisition of skill.

Following the International Congress of Sports Psychology in Rome of 1965, a National Society of Sports Psychologists was founded in Germany by Professor Kunath. At their yearly conferences they discuss current research and practices relating psychology to physical activity and sport. A number of texts and monographs have been published in Germany after World War II. In West Germany in 1957, Otto Neumann wrote *Sport Activity and Personality,* which was published in Munich; while in 1958 B. Wischmann published a monograph titled *The Problem of Courage in Physical Education.* (61), (106)

Sport Psychology in Russia

The beginnings of sport psychology in Russia may be traced in the writings of Dr. P. F. Lesgaft, a physician who in 1901 began to describe the possible psychological benefits to be derived from physical activity. (79) While pointing out the sensory-motor implications of voluntary movement, Lesgaft also suggested that physical education, if incorporated into educational programs for youth, could be helpful in the formation of the child's body image, his emotional well-being, his intellectual processes, as well as in the improvement of the self-control of motor functions. He also emphasized that the principal role of physical education in schools lies in the development of a number of perceptual processes, including the judgment of time, kinesthesis, the organization of visual space, and similar processes.

The first work that was carried out by psychologists on the topics suggested by Lesgaft's writings occurred following the Russian revolution in 1917. During the early 1920's a number of schools of physical education were established in Russia. Among the first to be established were the Institutes for Physical Culture in Moscow and Leningrad. They were organized like universities and contained several departments, one of which was called the Department of Psychology of Physical Education and Sports Activities.[1] Thus the beginnings of sport psychology in Russia are to be found within these departments.

Their first investigations were concerned with the analysis of motor skill and motor learning. Studies of reaction time are also to be found in the literature in 1925; among the first studies was one by Peter Roudik. (80) Other investigations by A. P. Netschajew, in 1926, studied the influence of physical education upon kinesthetic perception, memory, attention span, and imagination. (83) He also explored, during this early period, the manner in which sports activity exerted an influence upon the development of character.

Other early investigations contain data which attempted to illuminate relationships between physical activity and intellectual development on the part of school children. S. I. Tschutschmarew in 1928, for example, studied various motor-mental relationships. (83)

Researchers at Leningrad became concerned with the influence of participation in specific sports upon psychological development. For example, in 1929 the relationship of skiing to personality traits was investigated by A. C. Puni. (73)

These first studies in the psychology of sport were carried out without their being placed into any coherent over-all research plan. Each investigator conceived of his own topics and research programs. At the same time, the place of sport psychology within general psychology in Russia was not clearly defined. Additional problems revolved around the selec-

[1] Most of the material for this section was obtained from *Psychologie: Ein Lehrbuch fur Turnlehrer, Sportlehrer und Trainer* (Psychology: A Textbook for Physical Educators, Sports Teachers and Coaches), by P. A. Roudik, Chairman, Department of Psychology, Institute of Physical Culture, Moscow, Russia. Published by Volkseigener Verlag, Berlin, 1936.

tion of valid testing methodologies and the building of sophisticated equipment with which to carry out the investigations.

By 1930 the need for a concentrated research effort was felt among Russian physical educators, and a Scientific Research Institute for the Study of Physical Education was established within the Moscow Institute of Physical Culture. The Institute's purpose was not only to engage in psychological research, but also to study various physiological and mechanical parameters of physical activity. The first head of this institute was Professor W. W. Gorinewski, and the psychological research was coordinated by Professor Peter Roudik. (81) Initially this research was directed toward the exploration of various psychological evaluation techniques, including personality testing, intelligence testing, psychomotor testing, and the like. The establishment of this institute and its program of cooperative research between the several subdisciplines represented an important step forward in the scientific investigation of sport and physical activity within the Soviet Union.

The research emanating from this new institute was not only concerned with the manner in which physical activity contributed to educational objectives, but also with the manner in which exercise programs would contribute to or detract from the capacities of factory workers in Russia. As a result of some of this research, programs of industrial physical education were instituted in Russia, including the incorporation of "exercise breaks" within the factory, as well as the organization of recreational sports and games at the end of a working day.

Other investigations within the new institute were concerned with the physical qualities of members of the armed forces—for example, in the 1930's, studies determining whether balance was a critical factor in parachuting and in piloting aircraft.

In 1936, a reaction against intelligence and personality testing was discernible in Russia. Many felt that these testing and classification procedures were a form of discrimination which could result in unfairly limiting a child's opportunities at a rather early age. In many institutes these short-term tests were replaced by clinical evaluations occurring over prolonged periods of time. In the experimental laboratory, on the other hand, more emphasis was placed upon physiological psychology, particularly that based upon the principles discovered by Pavlov.

In the late 1930's, Professor Roudik evolved a general classification of sport psychology within which various studies of sport and physical activity might be placed. These subcategories included two main parts:

(a) The psychology of sports activities. Under this were placed two additional categories: one termed the general analysis of sports activities and the second was concerned with the analysis of specific sports.

(b) The second main part was termed the psychology of athletes, which also contained two subdivisions: specific abilities of athletes, and the second, general personality traits of athletes.

In addition, there were two other categories. One was concerned with the psychological basis of teaching and motor skill and the second was concerned with the training of superior athletes.

The primary aim of the studies within these categories was to obtain a deeper understanding of the superior athlete. This scheme was devised with the help of Professor Puni in Leningrad, and it aided in coordinating the efforts of sport psychologists all over Russia. Tbilisi, Moscow, and Leningrad now contain high-level training and research institutes concerned with the psychology of physical activity.

Among the topics seen in the Russian literature (83) at the close of the 1930's and the beginning of the 1940's were *The Specificity of Motives When Running Distances,* "Kinesthetic Awareness in Fencing," "The Perception of Time When Running," "Visual and Kinesthetic Perception in Gymnastics," "The Integration of Movement and Thought in Acrobatic Training," "The Specificity of Tactics in Various Sports," "Motor Learning in Gymnastics," "The Importance of Perceptual and Intellectual Components in Sports Activities," "The Role of Speech in Motor Learning," "Relationship Between Verbal Instructions and Visual Demonstrations in the Teaching of Skill," and "The Specificity of Motor Skill in Sports Activities." (83)

Despite the attempts to organize and focus entire research programs, the range of topics was extensive. The ingenuity of the experimenters and the depth of their thought were impressive. However, the data emanating from these studies were not usually treated with acceptable statistical methods.

From 1939 through the 1960's, a great deal of emphasis has been placed upon the study of pre-start tensions in athletes. In these investigations the physiologist and psychologist generally cooperated and monitored various physical indices of activation as athletes prepared for competition.

Over the years innumerable studies have been carried out to determine the psychological parameters of various sports. Emphasis has thus been placed upon the event and not directly upon the individual participant. Titles of these investigations reflect an interest in boxing, swimming, slalom skiing, wrestling, tennis, and soccer. The primary focus was upon what qualities of perception, emotion, attention, intelligence, and motor attributes were specific to various sports, and which attributes were relatively general and might satisfy the demands of several sports.

Various subtle "feelings" were also accorded attention by the Russians. Investigations of the "feeling" of the water by the swimmer, of the elusive "time sense" of runners, and of the tactual "ball feeling" by soccer and basketball players may be found throughout the Russian literature.

More global studies of athletes' motives and of athletic interests were also carried out during these years. From these studies more effective means by which a coach might train the "moral stamina" and will power of athletes were derived. Examples of the titles reflecting this interest include: "The Importance of Proper Exercises in Educating the Character," "The Psychological Analysis of Overcoming Obstacles in Sports," and "The Influence of Sports Participation upon Personality Development."

From 1936 to the present, a determined attempt was made to analyze the concept of will power. This rather nebulous concept was fragmented into courage, determination, tenacity, endurance, and self-discipline. (72)

More recently, materials from the previously described areas of study have been synthesized into guidelines for the psychological preparation of superior sportsmen. Thus by 1960 the importance of this general topic is reflected in the writings of Russian sport psychologists. Various case studies have also been carried out in which some of Russia's best athletes have been used as subjects. For example, the concentration time (time prior to jumping) of the high jumper, Valeri Brumel, was carefully clocked during the National Championship in Leningrad in 1963. (71) His "concentration time," when coupled with performance scores (i.e., height jumped), purportedly reveals important relationships between preperformance activation and optimum effort.

From the more general topic of will power, more emphasis has recently been placed upon specific techniques which may bring the athlete to optimum levels of activation prior to and during competition. The Schultz method of "Autogenne training," described in detail in Chapter 7, has been employed and coupled with electronic monitoring of measures of physical and psychological readiness.

More recently, emphasis has been placed upon research dealing with the psychology of small-group interaction. Despite the reluctance of Russian researchers to engage in investigations involving social psychology during the previous decades, observations of sports teams seemed to indicate that it is important to understand the quality of group interaction.

At the present time within the Soviet Union, three independent chairs of sport psychology have been established in the three large Institutes of Physical Culture (Moscow, Leningrad, and Tbilisi). Each department contains a large, well-equipped laboratory in which both simple and complex equipment may be found.

Periodically, All-Union Conferences of Sport Psychology are held at which experiments are discussed and new directions in research are planned. (82) In 1967 the National Society of Sport Psychology was founded in Russia, which at the present time consists of about one hundred and fifty members. Its membership roll contains, as participants, many of the more renowned psychologists in the country. Only psychologists who are active contributors to knowledge are admitted to the Society. Members of the Society not only work within their laboratories, but work closely with sports participants and their coaches.

In summary, sport psychology in Russia at the present time is primarily oriented toward investigations of the manner in which various physiological processes interact with psychological measures. The pioneering studies tended to pave the way to more contemporary investigations in which physical activity interacts within the total educational environment. Russian researchers are still interested in the concept of will power, but within recent years they seem to be redoubling their attempts to discover the emotional and intellectual basis of the concept.

Great concern is placed upon moral traits and character development. Special emphasis within some of these studies has been placed upon the ideological and political ramifications of sports participation.

A great deal of time is taken in carrying out careful observations of the behavior of many of the superior athletes in Russia. The data emanating from these observations, together with the information previously obtained concerning the psychological demands of various sports, purportedly combine to aid coaches and physical educators in producing highly motivated and well-performing athletes.

Psychology and Sports in the United States

Philosophical and experimental interest in the relationship of various psychological variables to motor activity may be found in the writings of several physical educators in the United States around the turn of the century. The early beginnings of a scientific approach to physical activity usually involved an examination of various physiological variables. Clark Hetherington, Jesse Ferring Williams, and others in the early part of the 1900's began to suggest that physical activity could do more for children than simply make small muscles larger. (40), (105) Before the turn of the century experimental psychologists had begun to explore movement behavior. Between the 1890's and the 1930's, studies by Woodworth and others pointed to the widespread interest in kinesthesis. Guthrie proposed a contiguity theory of learning whose basis was the chaining together of movement responses, while reference to the "Great God Kinesthesis" may be found in the proceedings of one of the early psychological conventions. (108), (37)

Accompanying philosophical writings in the 1920's and the 1930's were investigations in some of the basic problems connected with motor learning. Laboratories were established in several universities by the 1930's (the University of Illinois, Penn State, Iowa, and others). In 1928 a text was published, authored by Coleman Griffith. It was titled *Psychology of Coaching* and dealt with a scientific approach to instruction in various sports. (35) Dr. Griffith headed the motor learning laboratory at the University of Illinois, while Dr. John Lawther at Penn State and Clarence Ragsdale at the University of Wisconsin established other laboratories in physical education departments in the 1930's. Ragsdale's book titled *The Psychology of Motor Learning* was one of the first in the United States. (74)

In 1930, another significant step was taken to promote research within the profession of physical education. *The Research Quarterly,* a journal devoted to the publication of research in physical education, was established by the American Physical Education Association, with Elmer D. Mitchell as its first editor.

During these same years, experimental psychologists in departments of psychology throughout the country continued to carry out studies dealing with motor learning and motor performance, but often their use of motor tasks in their experiments was only incidental to their primary purposes. Snoody, for example, employed the pursuit rotor to study what he termed "mental growth." (94)

Research in motor activity during World War II often dealt with the needs of the armed forces. And several governmental research programs were instituted dealing with the skills needed in flight training. (25) The text titled *The Assessment of Men* describes a similar program in which a number of perceptual-motor tasks were employed in a program evaluating the resourcefulness of men entering the Office of Strategic Services. (66)

Following World War II, activity continued in Physical Education departments and within an emerging field termed Human Factors Research, in which Psychology aligned itself with Engineering in order to solve problems usually involving some kind of man-machine relationship. Two Ph.D.'s in Psychology worked diligently in Physical Education departments and spurred research in motor performance and motor learning. Dr. Arthur Slater-Hammel at the University of Indiana carried out research in a number of topics, including the differences between kinesthetic perception of athletes and that of nonathletes. (92) Dr. Franklin M. Henry at the University of California at Berkeley also established a productive research laboratory which not only contributed to knowledge about reaction time, movement speed, and motor learning, but also produced a number of excellent doctoral students who established laboratories at the University of California at Davis, at the University of Iowa, and at other locations throughout the United States. (39)

During the first fifty years of the twentieth century, little direct work took place among coaches, psychologists, and superior athletes. John Lawther, however, published a book titled the *Psychology of Coaching*. (52) In general, coaches in the United States might talk vaguely of "psyching up" their athletes, while making few attempts to obtain and use available findings and literature.

During the 1930's, 1940's, and 1950's doctoral dissertations were occasionally written in which athletes were compared to nonathletes using some measure of personality and/or perceptual-motor behavior, but no coordinated and sustained research effort was made to understand the superior athlete. The studies that were completed usually represented piecemeal efforts, and neither the term "athlete" nor the evaluative tools employed (personality scales and the like) were well standardized.

By the end of the 1950's, despite the seeming lack of concern earlier for applied problems which would have focused attention upon the superior athlete, a great deal of evidence had been collected concerning the nature of motor activity and motor learning. One of the more sophisticated programs was conducted by a psychologist working in an Air Force research program in Texas from 1952 to 1956. Dr. Edwin Fleishman, from the early 1950's to the present time, has carried out innumerable studies, often employing factor-analytic techniques which permitted the identification of various perceptual-motor domains. His more recent investigations have centered upon analysis of factors important during various stages of learning skills. Factor analyses within this general area have proven to be an important contribution to our understanding of the importance of various factors during the initial, middle, and final portions of a learning curve. (25), (24), (26)

At the same time the literature produced by physical educators began to suggest an increase in motor learning and movement behavior. Articles dealing with the psychology of physical activity appeared more frequently in *The Research Quarterly.* Several physical educators began to publish their work in psychological journals in the United States, including *Perceptual and Motor Skills,* edited by Drs. Robert and Carol Ammons, psychologists at the University of Montana.

In the 1960's, several texts appeared summarizing some of the research literature dealing with the psychology of motor activity. Cratty, in 1964, published *Movement Behavior and Motor Learning,* a text designed for graduate students. (21) A subsequent book, *Psychology and Physical Activity,* by the same author presented a basic outline of information directed toward the coach and teachers in training. (20) In 1967 two other texts intended for the student of physical education appeared on the bookshelves. Joseph Oxendine of Temple University in Pennsylvania wrote *Psychology and Motor Learning* and Robert Singer, from the University of Illinois at Normal, Illinois, wrote *Motor Learning and Human Performance,* both excellent contributions to the literatuure. (67), (88)

In 1962, two clinical psychologists at San Jose State College in San Jose, California, Thomas Tutko and Bruce Ogilvie, began to utilize various personality scales in studying the personality traits of various athletic teams in the San Francisco area. During the next several years their services were solicited by several university and college teams in several sports, and they spent a great deal of their time advising coaches concerning the personality dynamics of their charges. Their studies have included assessments of Olympic swimmers, professional and amateur football and baseball players, and athletes in other sports as well. In 1966, as a result of their observations, they published a text titled *Problem Athletes and How to Handle Them.* (62) It is believed that these are the only two men in the United States at the present time whose primary research interests center around superior athletes. Others in the United States have either carried out only one or two investigations in this area, have concentrated their efforts upon school children, or upon basic problems in motor learning and motor behavior.

Several psychiatrists during the late 1960's have become interested in sport and the psychodynamics of athletes. A text titled *Motivations in Play, Games, and Sports* (93) contains essays by about fifty psychiatrists and others, most of whom attempt to describe the manner in which the human ego and man's sporting activities interact.

One of the best texts in English dealing wtih the athlete was also produced in the 1960's. Entitled *The Madness in Sports,* this excellent publication was written by Arnold Beisser, a psychiatrist who was a former sports writer and champion tennis player. (7) Now confined to a wheel chair, Dr. Beisser's writing style and deep insights should provide many athletes with added understanding of their feelings when competing, and also when their competitive days have ended. One of the primary themes running through the pages of Beisser's book is the suggestion that it is imperative to replace the personality support provided to college athletes by their participation in sports with other means of expression when their bodies and talents can no longer serve them in good stead. His case studies of a basketball player, tennis player, and football player, it is believed, are classics, and deserve serious consideration by all those connected in any way with superior athletes.

In 1965, at the invitation of Ferrucio Antonelli, thirty-five physical educators journeyed to Rome to attend the First International Congress of Sport Psychology. While there, under the leadership of Arthur Slater-Hammel and others, they formed the North American Society of Psychology in Sport and Physical Activity.[2] Upon returning home, meetings were held during the next two years on the day prior to national conventions of the American Association of Health, Physical Education, and Recreation in Las Vegas, Nevada, and in St. Louis, Missouri, in 1967 and in 1968.

By 1968 the North American Society of Sports Psychology had grown to two hundred members, and in November of that year it held the Second International Congress of Sports Psychology with the American Association of Health, Physical Education, and Recreation being a co-

---

[2] The somewhat cumbersome title was formulated inasmuch as it was obvious that most of the membership was not primarily interested in superior athletes, but rather in more general parameters of motor activity and the educational implications of movement in school physical education programs.

sponsor. Over two hundred behavioral scientists from sixteen countries attended the four-day meeting, and over one hundred papers were read. Eight major addresses from leading psychologists and psychiatrists throughout the world were also presented.

At present there is a marked trend in physical education programs within colleges and universities to include courses in motor learning, psychology of physical activity, and other courses with similar titles. Dr. Lawrence Locke at Columbia, in 1966, established a Ph.D. program in motor learning, and the first graduates are now emerging. Several other universities throughout the country encourage specialization at the doctoral level in the psychology of motor activity. At the 1968 St. Louis Convention of Health, Physical Education, and Recreation thirty research papers were read which contained references to the physiology of physical activity, while forty-three papers dealt with psychological parameters.

There is an increased concern in many research laboratories in physical education about various mental-motor relationships. Spurred by the Joseph P. Kennedy Foundation, as well as by theoreticians in the United States who have claimed that motor activities may remediate a variety of problems of atypical children, some physical educators have been encouraged to conduct research in educational problems dealing with mental retardation and neurological impairment. Dr. Lawrence Rarick at the Universities of Wisconsin and of California has been one of the leading researchers in this area of investigation. (75)

A concentrated interest in the psychology of sport and of the superior athlete received only cursory attention in the United States as the 1960's drew to a close. Perhaps this text, together with a consideration of some of the foreign studies, may encourage more fruitful communication between coaches, researchers, clinical psychologists, and physicians in the United States such as has been occurring in Europe and in other parts of the world.

Sport Psychology in Czechoslovakia [3]

The first glimmering of an interest in the psychology of physical activity in Czechoslovakia was seen in a doctoral dissertation completed in 1928 by Augustin Pechlat at Charles University. (70) (Pechlat's dissertation

[3] The majority of the material in this section was obtained from *The Psychological Basis of Physical Education* by M. Vanek, State Pedagogical Publisher, Prague, 1963.

was published in 1948 in his memory.) This dissertation outlined the manner in which physical exercise might contribute to the psychological development of the individual. In the middle 1930's, a Czech athlete, Karel Chudoba (17), after studying in the United States, returned to his native country and wrote a monograph dealing with the psychological preparation of the athlete. Whereas the initial document by Pechlat was speculative and philosophical in nature, this latter approach by Chudoba incorporated ideas obtained from the experimental laboratories of America.

In 1887 an institute for the training of physical educators was established in Prague and staffed by visiting professors from the sciences on the faculty of Charles University, and by part-time coaches who taught courses in teaching methods. Following World War II, the institute obtained its own faculty. In 1950 a lecturer was engaged to give courses about the psychological basis of physical activity and sport.

Although plans for a university-level Institute for Physical Education were formulated in 1938, they were not finalized until 1953 due to the interruption of the war, when another Institute of Physical Education and Sport was established with the help and encouragement of Russian sport scientists (psychologists, physicians, and educators).

This second institute contained a subfaculty of theoreticians and psychologists. Two psychologists, A. Stransky (98) and M. Brichcin (11), began teaching courses in the psychology of sport at the new institute. The first experimental laboratory devoted to the study of problems involving the psychology of physical activity was also founded at that time in this new institute.

In 1958 the older training school and the new institute merged and were incorporated into the faculty of Charles University. This organizational change resulted in a regression of the psychology of sport, as only one staff member from the two institutes was retained, while the others went to the regular faculty of psychology at Charles University.

A similar process of development, from teacher training schools to the university structure, occurred in Bratislava, where a chair of Sport Psychology was established in the faculty of physical education of Commenius University. The first and present occupant of this chair is Ivan Macak. (54)

Counteracting this apparent academic setback, however, was the growth of the National Society of Sport Psychologists which had been established in Prague in 1954, and whose rolls now include fifteen members. This society was organized within the Scientific Council of the National Committee of Physical Education and Sport. The membership included psychologists interested in motor behavior, theoretical psychologists, research psychologists, physiological psychologists, clinical psychologists, as well as individuals responsible for the teaching of psychology courses to physical educators in colleges in Prague, Bratislava, Brno, and Olomouc.

During the formative years of the Society, a number of speakers were invited, and seminars were held during which various members could present their work and have it criticized. The first studies carried out by the membership concerned general topics of motor skill, motor learning, motor development of children, transfer of training, the carry-over values of physical education, and similar topics. Additionally, the membership was interested in the analyses of various sports with respect to their psychological parameters.

Seminars were instituted by the Society which would appeal to coaches. Numerous lectures and discussions were held with coaches throughout the country since 1954. Periodically newsletters in sport psychology are mailed to coaches. Thus to an increasing degree the focus of the Society became fixed upon the needs of coaches dealing with superior athletes. This interest in superior athletic attainment was partially influenced by the ideological, social, and political importance attached to the attainment of superior athletes within the Czechoslovakian society. In addition, many of the psychologists in the Society began to believe that basic information concerning the performance of men under stress could best be studied by investigating the psychological environment in which the superior athlete resided. It was also felt by some of the scholars that a study of the superior athlete could reveal important lessons which would enable them to better understand the nature of the psychological stresses impinging upon lower-level performers.

The first studies of the superior athlete centered around the concept of "will power." Gradually, however, it was found that the concept of "will power" is a multi-faceted problem, and thus studies in various subtopics were undertaken. A second main theme in these investigations dealt with levels of aspiration in sports activities. A third area of concern centered around the topic of personality of superior athletes and personality differences between participants in various sports. Attention was also directed toward the psychological preparation of athletes.

The work of the Sport Psychology Society became recognized throughout the country by coaches and by officials on the National Committee of Physical Education and Sport and on the Czech Olympic Committee. One member of the Society participated in a Conference for Sports Sciences in Tokyo in 1964, lecturing on the "Personality of the Athlete." Following this meeting the psychologist remained as an observer attached to the Czech Olympic team.

As the next Olympics was to be held in a mile-high city, Czechoslovakian psychologists, following the 1964 Olympics, were invited to an increasing degree to study the influence of altitude upon performance. Invitations to investigate this altitudinal stress upon superior athletes were extended by members of the National Olympic Committee and by the National Committee of Physical Education and Sport.

The details of this pre-Olympic training, evaluation, and testing prior to the Mexican Olympics are given in Chapter 11. A team of psychologists was invited to work closely with the nation's superior athletes during this period, and one of their members was named to accompany the team to Mexico City.

The psychological investigations of motor activity and of athletes had been carried out up to this time in laboratories. From 1964 to 1968, in Czechoslovakia, however, it was attempted to apply what was known about motor performance and learning, personality, and psychotherapy directly to participants in athletic contests, and thus to attempt to improve their performance.

In Czechoslovakia, contemporary work includes investigations of the personality of coaches, as well as various sociometric studies of the interactions of large and small groups within sports teams.

In both Bratislava and in Ceske-Budejovices, offices have been established by the National Society of Sport Psychology to which coaches and athletes may come and consult with physicians and psychologists concerning their problems. (47) These offices are open two days a week, and the program is financed by the National Committee of Physical Education and Sport and by local governmental districts.

In 1968, special chairs of Sport Psychology and Pedagogy were instituted in Charles University in Prague, and at the University of Commenius in Bratislava. Graduate psychology students at Charles University may choose to specialize in sport psychology during their final year of study. From this group it is expected that the future generations of sport psychologists will emerge in Czechoslovakia.

Contemporary Trends in Sport Psychology [4]

Each country in the world, due to cultural differences, emphasizes different aspects of the psychology of sport and physical activity. One important unifying event was the 1965 Congress of Sport Psychology organized by Professor Ferruccio Antonelli, a psychiatrist from the Catholic University in Rome. (2), (3), (4)

Although the authors are not in direct contact with all the various national societies, through their attendance at international meetings and through correspondence they are aware of some of the current trends in sport psychology throughout the world today. In many countries the various societies seem to be advancing in membership and in the quality of research and service they render to physical education and to sport. In some countries there is a natural starting point at the university level for the formation and activities of these societies. The training of these physical educators includes psychological preparation. In other countries where this is absent, the formation and activities of these societies are carried out with more difficulty.

In France there is a laboratory of sport psychology at the Normal School of Physical Education (*Ecole normale supérieure d'éducation physique*). This laboratory is headed by Professor E. Hiriartborde, a psychologist. His special interest is in the study of rhythm. (41) Topics researched include the ability of humans to reproduce rhythms and the neurological basis of rhythmic activity.

One of the standard texts used in France at the present time was written in 1955 by Loisel and is titled *The Psychological Bases of Physical Education.* (53) Professor Coche's text titled *Manual of Pedagogy Applied in Physical Education,* a 1948 text, is also found in the physical training schools of France. (18)

The French Society of Sport Psychology was founded in 1967. At the present time it has about two hundred members on its rolls. The membership includes psychologists, physical educators, psychiatrists, as well as physical therapists. One of its members, Andre Bouvet, is working with the French Olympic skiers; another member, Eric De Winter, is currently

[4] Some of the material for this section was obtained from "Sports Psychology in the Literature," by Dr. Morgan A. Olsen, in *Proceedings* of the First International Congress of Sport Psychology, Ferruccio Antonelli (ed.), Rome, 1965, pp. 1220–84.

teaching courses in the autogenic training of athletes, and still another, Michel Bouvet, has written extensively in the area of motivation. (9), (8) Two recent books have been written by Georges Rioux and Raymond Chappuis. One is titled *The Team in Group Sports* (*L'Equipe dans les sports collectifs*), while the second, *The Psycho-Pedagogical Bases of Body Education*, contains both theory and practice in dealing with various psychological variables as they influence physical education and sports performance. (77), (76)

In England three workers have been productive within recent years. Kane's several studies of the personalities of superior athletes are reviewed in Chapter 3. (43) He is a member of the managing council of the International Society of Sport Psychology. Barbara Knapp's excellent book titled *Skill in Sport* was published in 1963, and is currently being used as a text in a number of colleges and universities in Britain and in the United States. (46) James Oliver's research dealing with the effects of motor activity upon the intelligence of retarded children attracted worldwide attention in the 1950's. (64)

In Italy, Antonelli's text titled *The Psychology and Psychopathology of Sport* (1960) is a prominent guide to the literature. (2), (3) The Italian society continues to evidence growth, and numbers among its three hundred members some of the more prominent psychiatrists, physical educators, sport physicians, and psychologists in Italy.

Professor J. M. Cagigal of the National Ministry of Physical Education and Sport in Madrid is one of the leading members of the Spanish society. Dr. Jose Ferre-Hombrevella of Barcelona, a psychiatrist, is also prominent in the organization of the Spanish Society of Sport Psychology and is the first secretary of the managing council of the International Society of Sport Psychology. Sport psychologists in Spain are primarily interested in the personality dynamics and group dynamics of athletic teams.

In Bulgaria there is an Institute of Physical Culture in Sophia that trains physical educators at the university level. The Institute, established with the encouragement of the Soviet Union after World War II, contains a research laboratory and a chair of Sport Psychology presently held by Professor Ema Geron. (31) The primary topics in which this group is interested include the psychological preparation of the superior athlete, the influence of altitude upon performance, and other research dealing with emotions and will power. Professor Geron and her assistants have published an extremely helpful book outlining experimental methods used in the field and in the laboratory that are applicable to sport psychology. (32)

The Bulgarian Society of Sport Psychology, similar to the one in Czechoslovakia, has a membership which must meet professional qualifications for admission. Several members of the society worked with the Bulgarian Olympic team prior to the 1968 Olympics in their pre-acclimitization training.

In Romania the chair in sport psychology is held by Professor Michail Epuran of the Institute of Physical Culture in Bucharest. (23) The Romanian Society of Sport Psychologists consists of about twenty-five members, and their main research interests center around general research in motor learning, as well as topics relating to the preparation of their superior athletes.

In Switzerland work in sport psychology is being carried out in the E.T.S. School of Physical Education in Maglingen. Research and lectures dealing with the personality of the athlete as well as with relationships between mental capacity and physical performance are being carried out at Maglingen by Guido Schilling and his colleagues.

In Warsaw, Poland, the Academy of Physical Education has a chair of Sport Psychology, as well as extensive research facilities. Their primary focus is upon operant conditioning of motor responses, as well as on various problems concerning small groups centering around athletic teams. The National Society of Sport Psychology, founded in 1967, at the present time numbers about forty members. This membership is composed of physical educators, sociologists, psychologists, and psychiatrists, including professors Andrzej Wohl, Wiktoria Nawrocka, Erazm Wasilewski, Eugenius Geblewicz, and Maria Geblewiczowa. (107), (60), (103), (28), (29)

In Hungary there is a National Society of Sport Psychology. Dr. Arato, a Hungarian psychiatrist, has been interested in psychotherapy and the use of hypnosis with superior athletes. (5)

In Belgrade, Yugoslavia, Dr. Momirovic directs a laboratory in the Institute of Physical Culture. The research program in Yugoslavia is focused upon the psychological preparation of superior athletes and the factors which contribute to outstanding sport performance. (57)

Dr. Morgan Olsen of Norway and Dr. Tobjorn Stockfelt of Stockholm, Sweden, are currently organizing a Society of Sport Psychology in the Scandinavian countries. (65), (96), (97) This society will include members from Finland, Denmark, as well as Sweden and Norway. Stockfelt has been analyzing the intelligence of superior skiers and swimmers, and has also carried out research dealing with motivation.

In Holland the psychologist Professor F. J. J. Buytendijk has proven to be a prolific writer. In 1928 he spoke about the psychology of sport at a scientific meeting which preceded the Olympics in Amsterdam. The textbooks he has published since that time include: *The Nature and the Sense of Play*, 1933; *Soccer, A Psychological Study*, 1953; and *General Theory of Human Posture and Movement*, 1956. (13), (14), (15)

In Brazil the National Society is led by Ribeiro Da Silva, a lawyer and psychologist who is also a member of the managing Council of the International Society. Other groups in Argentina and Chile are also contemplating organizing societies. Their primary concern is with soccer.

The Japanese Society has been functioning since the end of World War II. At the present time the Society is concerned with a variety of problems including motor learning, physiological and neurological bases of motor activity, and similar topics. Their experimental methods are often similar to those used in the United States. Dr. Kinji Ikegami represented his country at the Second International Congress of Sport in Washington, D.C. (43) Professor Ohkawa (3) from Tokyo, one of the main speakers at the pre-scientific meeting preceding the Tokyo Olympics in 1964 (63), wrote his paper on the personality of athletes, as compared with nonathletes. The president of the Japanese Society is Professor Iwao Matsuda from Tokyo. (55)

The most recent significant event that has influenced the course of sport psychology was the Second International Congress of Sport Psychology held in Washington, D.C., following the 1968 Mexican Olympics. Over one hundred papers were given and the attendance exceeded two hundred. Present were psychiatrists, psychologists, physical educators, and educators from sixteen countries. At the present time the president of the International Society of Sport Psychology places its total world membership at more than 1400.

Summary

It is apparent that sport psychology is one of the younger disciplines within the larger area of psychology. In some countries the psychology of sports is accorded respect by coaches, physicians, psychologists, and by educators. However, in other countries members of other related scientific disciplines are unaware of the interests of their countrymen in this emerging and vital area of knowledge.

Sport psychology at the present time consists of information from the following three general areas: (a) information about general motor behavior, motor learning, and motor development; (b) theoretical speculation and research data dealing with the psychological preparation of the superior athlete, with various psychological subareas consisting of motivation, personality dynamics, pre-competition training, and the like; (c) research and writings dealing with the social psychology of team and individual sports.

REFERENCES

1. Allport, G. W. *Personality: A Psychological Interpretation.* New York: Holt, Rinehart, 1937.
2. Antonelli, F. *La Valutazione Psicologica dell'Atleta* (The Psychological Evaluation of the Athlete). Rome: Scientiche Leonardo, 1964.
3. Antonelli, F. *Psicologia e Psicopathologia dello Sport* (The Psychology and Psychopathology of Sport). Rome: Scientiche Leonardo, 1960.
4. Antonelli, F. (ed.). *Proceedings,* First International Congress of Sport Psychology, Rome: F.M.S.I., 1965.
5. Arato, O. "Quelques Remarques sur la Psychopathologie et Psychotherapie des Competiteurs, du point de vue de la neuropsychiatrie pratique" (Some Discussions of the Psychopathology and Psychotherapy of Athletes, from the point of view of Neuropsychiatry). *Proceedings,* First International Congress of Sports Psychology, F. Antonelli (ed.), Rome, 1965.
6. Barth, B. *Willens- und Charakterbildung durch Leibesubungen* (Will Power and Character Formation Through Physical Exercises). Berlin, 1912.
7. Beisser, A. *The Madness in Sports.* New York: Appleton-Century-Crofts, 1967.
8. Bouvet, M. "Recherches sur la Motivation du Sportif" (Research in the Motivation of Athletes). *Proceedings,* First International Congress of Sport Psychology, F. Antonelli (ed.), Rome, 1965.
9. Bouvet, A.; Digo, R.; and Missenard, A. "Quinze ans d'activites Medico-Psychologiques au sein de la Federation Française de Ski" (Fifteen Years of Medical-Psychological Activity in the French Ski Federation). *Proceedings,* First International Congress of Sports Psychology, F. Antonelli (ed.), Rome, 1965.
10. Bowditch, H. P., and Southard, W. F. "A Comparison of Sight and Touch." *J. Physiol.,* 3:232–54, 1882.

11. Brichcin, M. "Problem Volniho Usili" (Problem of Volitional Effort). *Ceskoslovenska Psychologie* (Czechoslovakian Psychology), 1960.
12. Buehler, K. *Die Geistige Entwicklung des Kindes* (The Mental Development of the Child). Vienna, 1918.
13. Buytendijk, F. J. J. *Wesen und Sinn des Spieles. Das Spielen der Menschen und der Tiere als Erscheinungsform der Lebenstriebe* (The Nature and the Sense of Play. The Play in Humans and Animals as a Phenomenon of the Drives of Life). Berlin, 1933.
14. Buytendijk, F. J. J. *Das Fussballspiel. Eine Psychologische Studie* (Soccer, A Psychological Study). Wuerzburg: Werkbund, 1953.
15. Buytendijk, F. J. J. *Allgemeine Theorie der Menschlichen Haltung und Bewegung* (General Theory of Human Posture and Movement). Berlin: Springer, 1956.
16. Cerny, J. *Fotball je hra* (The Game of Soccer). Prague: Czechoslovakian author, 1968.
17. Chudoba, K. *Psychologie treninku* (Psychology of Training). Brno, 1932.
18. Coche, A. *Manual de Pedagogie Applique a l'Education Physique* (Manual of Pedagogy Applied in Physical Education). Paris, 1948.
19. Comenius, J. A. *Didactica Magna* (Great Didactics). Prague, 1930.
20. Cratty, Bryant J. *Psychology and Physical Activity*. Englewood Cliffs, N.J.: Prentice-Hall, 1967.
21. Cratty, Bryant J. *Movement Behavior and Motor Learning*. Philadelphia: Lea and Febiger, 2nd ed., 1967.
22. de Coubertin, P. *Essays de Psychologie Sportive* (The Essays on Sports Psychology). Paris: Lausanne, 1913.
23. Epuran, M. *Die Psychologie der Korpererziehung* (The Psychology of Physical Education). Bucharest, 1962.
24. Fleishman, Edwin A., and Parker, J. F. "Factors in the Retention and Relearning of Perceptual-Motor Skills." *J. Exp. Psych.,* **64**:215–26, 1962.
25. Fleishman, Edwin A., and Hempel, Walter E., Jr. "Changes in Factor Structure of a Complex Psychomotor Test as a Function of Practice." *Psychometrics,* **19**:239–52, 1954.
26. Fleishman, Edwin A., and Rich, S. "Role of Kinesthetic and Spatial-Visual Abilities in Perceptual-Motor Learning." *J. Exp. Psych.,* **66**:6–11, 1963.
27. Freud, S. *Hemmung, Sumtom und Angst* (Inhibition, Symptom and Anxiety). Vienna, 1926.
28. Geblewicz, E. "Postawa Sportowa" (Sporting Attitude). *Wych. Fiz. Sport,* Warsaw, 4, 1960.
29. Geblewiczowa, M. "Wplpw Emocjonalnego Aspektu Sygnalu Ostrzegawczego na Czas Reakcji Prostej" (The Influence of the Emotional Aspect of an Alarm Signal upon the Time of a Single Reaction). *Wych. Fiz. Sport,* Warsaw, 3, 10, 1959.
30. Geron, E. *Psychology, A Textbook for Students in V.I.F.* (Higher Institute of Physical Culture). Sofia: Medicina, Fizkultura, 1961.
31. Geron, E.; Popov, N.; and Dimitrova, S. *Methods for Psychological Investigations.* Sofia: Medicina, Fitzkultura, 1963.

32. Giese, F. *Geist im Sport* (Spirit in Sport). Bern, 1925.
33. Giese, F. *Die Psychotechnik in der Korpererziehung* (Psychotechniques in Physical Education). Bern, 1928.
34. Giese, F. *Korperseele, Gedanken uber Personliche Gestaltung* (Soul of the Body, Ideas on Personality Formation). Munich, 1924.
35. Griffith, Coleman R. *Psychology of Coaching, A Study of Coaching Methods from the Point of View of Psychology.* New York: C. Scribner's Sons, 1928.
36. Groos, K. *Das Spiel, zwei Vortraege: 1. der Lebenswert des Spiels; 2. das Spiel als Katharsis* (Play: 1. The Value of Play in Life; 2. Play as Catharsis). Jena, 1922.
37. Guthrie, E. R. *The Psychology of Learning.* New York: Harper and Row, 1935.
38. Hackensmith, C. W. *History of Physical Education.* New York: Harper and Row, 1966.
39. Henry, F. M. "Increased Response Latency for Complicated Movements, and a Memory Drum Theory of Neuromotor Reactions." *Res. Quart.,* **31**:43–53, 1952.
40. Hetherington, Clark. *School Program in Physical Education.* Yonkers-on-Hudson, New York: World Book Co., 1922.
41. Hiriartborde, E. *Les Aptitudes Rythmiques: Etude de Psychologie Differentielle* (The Rhythmic Aptitudes: Study in Differential Psychology). Paris, 1964.
42. Ikegami, K. "Character and Personality Changes in the Athlete." Paper read to Second International Congress of Sport Psychology, Washington, D.C., 1968.
43. Kane, J. "Personality and Physical Attributes." Paper read to Second International Congress of Sport Psychology, Washington, D.C., 1968.
44. Klemm, O. *Gedanken uber Leibesübungen* (Ideas About Physical Education). Munich: Neve Psychogische Studien, Bd. 5 (New Psychological Studies, Band 5), 1931.
45. Klemm, O. *Zwolf Leitsatze su Einer Psychologie der Leibesübungen in Motorik von Krueger, F.* (Twelve Principles in the Psychology of Physical Exercise Leading into the Motorics of F. Krueger). Munich, 1938.
46. Knapp, Barbara. *Skill in Sport.* London: Routledge and Kegan Paul, 1963.
47. Kodym, M. "Sportovni Psychologicka Poradna" (Sports Psychological Office). *Teorie a Praxe Telesne Vychovy,* Prague, **13**:7, 1965.
48. Kratky, F. *Dejiny Telesne Vychovy* (The History of Physical Education). Prague: State Pedagogical Publisher, 1962.
49. Krueger, F., and Klemm, O. *Motorik* (Motorics). Munich, 1938.
50. Kunath, P. *Psychologie. Anleitung fur das Fernstudium* (Psychology, Introduction for Extramural Studies). Leipzig, 1963.
51. Lawther, John D. *The Learning of Physical Skills.* Englewood Cliffs, N.J.: Prentice-Hall, 1968.
52. Lawther, John D. *Psychology of Coaching.* Englewood Cliffs, N.J.: Prentice-Hall, 1951.

53. Loisel, E. *Bases Psychologiques de l'Education Physique* (The Psychological Bases of Physical Education). Paris: Bourrelier, 1955.
54. Macak, I. *Psychologia Sportu* (Sports Psychology). Bratislava, 1962.
55. Matsuda, Iwao. *Modern Psychology of Sports.* Modern Series of Physical Education and Sports, 1, 1968.
56. Meinel, K. *Bewegungslehre* (Movement Theory). Berlin, 1960.
57. Momirovic, K. "Psiholoske Pripreme Olimpijske Reprezentacije" (The Psychological Preparation of Olympic Athletes). *Tel. Vaspitanje Sport Prak.*, Belgrade, **5**:2, 1964.
58. Mueller, S. "Erfolg und Misserfolg als Sport Psychologisches Problem" (Success and Failure in Sport as a Psychological Problem). *Theorie und Praxis der Korperkultur,* Leipzig, **70**:3, 1961.
59. Mueller, S. "Nervositat Vorstartzustand bei Boxern" (Nervousness Pre-start Tensions in Boxers). *Theorie und Praxis der Korperkultur,* Leipzig, **10**:8, 1961.
60. Nawrocka, W. "Z badan nad Osobowoscia Sportowcow" (From Studies of Athletes' Personality). Kultura Fizicna, Warsaw, **16**, 1963.
61. Neumann, O. *Sport und Personlichkeit. Versuch Einer Psychologischen Diagnostik mit Deutung der Personlichkeit des Sportlers* (Sport Activity and Personality. The Use of a Psychological Assessment to Evaluate the Personality of the Athlete). Munich, 1957.
62. Ogilvie, B. C., and Tutko, T. A. *Problem Athletes and How to Handle Them.* London: Pelham Books, Ltd., 1966.
63. Ohkawa, N. "A Study of General Traits and Syndromes of First-Class Sportsmen in Japan." *Sport and Sciences,* Tokyo, 1964.
64. Oliver, J. "The Effect of Physical Conditioning Exercises and Activities on the Mental Characteristics of Educationally Sub-normal Boys." *Brit. J. Ed. Psych.*, **28**:155–65, 1958.
65. Olsen, M. A. "Sports Psychology in the Literature." *Proceedings,* First International Congress of Sport Psychology, F. Antonelli (ed.), Rome, 1965.
66. O.S.S. (Office of Strategic Services). *The Assessment of Men.* New York: Holt, Rinehart, 1948.
67. Oxendine, Joseph B. *Psychology and Motor Learning.* New York: Appleton-Century-Crofts, 1968.
68. Ozolin, N. G. "Sovremenaja Sistema Sportivnoj Trenirovky" (The System of Contemporary Sports Training). *Mesdunarodnaja Naucno-Metodices-kaja Konferencija po Problemam Sportivnoj Trenirovky* (Proceedings of the International Scientific-Methodological Conference of Sports Training), Moscow, Vol. 1, 1962.
69. Pavlov, I. P. *Sebrane Spisy* (Collected Publications). Prague, 1952.
70. Pechlat, A. *Psychologie Telesnych Cviceni* (Psychology of Physical Exercises). Prague, 1948.
71. Petrovic, V. K. "Bezprostredni Psychologicka Priprava Lehkych Atletu (Skokanu a Vrhacu) pred Vlastnim Zavodem v Soutezich" (Psychological Preparation of Track-and-Field Competitors [Jumpers and Throwers]

Immediately Before the Competition), translated from Russian into Czech, *Teorie a Praxe Telesne Vychovy*. Prague, **15**:9, 1967.

72. Puni, A. C. *Vospitanije Voli Sportsmena* (Sportsmen's Will Power). Leningrad, 1958.

73. Puni, A. C. *Abriss der Sportpsychologie* (The Outline of Sports Psychology). Berlin: Volkseigener Verlag, 1962.

74. Ragsdale, C. E. *The Psychology of Motor Learning*. Ann Arbor: Edward Bros. Press, 1930.

75. Rarick, L. G., and Broadhead, G. D. "The Effects of Individualized Versus Group-oriented Physical Education Programs on Selected Parameters of the Development of Educable Mentally Retarded and Minimally Brain Injured Children." *U.S. Office of Ed. Monograph*, Contract OEG-0-071097-1760, 1968.

76. Rioux, G., and Chappuis, R. *Les Bases Psycho-Pedagogiques de l'Education Corporelle* (The Psycho-Pedagogical Bases of Body Education). Paris: Librairie Philosophique J. Vrin, 1968.

77. Rioux, G., and Chappuis, R. *L'Equipe dans les Sports Collectifs* (The Team in Group Sports). Paris: Librairie Philosophique J. Vrin, 1968.

78. Roback, A. A. *A History of American Psychology*. New York: Collier Books, 1964.

79. Roudik, P. A. *Psychologie: Ein Lehrbuch fur Turnlehrer, Sportlehrer und Trainer* (Psychology: A Textbook for Physical Educators, Sports Teachers and Coaches). Berlin: Volkseigener Verlag, 1936.

80. Roudik, P. A. "Vlijanie Muskolnoj Raboty na Process Reakcii" (The Influence of Muscle Activity on Reaction Time). *Trudy Gcilfk* (Works of the Central Institute of Physical Culture), Moscow, 1925.

81. Roudik, P. A. "Ein Verfahren zur Psychologischen Untersuchung von Korpererzihern" (The Directions for Psychological Investigations by Physical Educators), *Forschungsmethodik und Wertungsprinzipien fur den Einfluss von Leibesuebungen* (The Research Methods and Principles of Evaluation of the Influences of Physical Exercises). Moscow: Statsverlag fur Medizinische Literatur, 1930.

82. Roudik, P. A. "Allunionskonferez der USSR uber Psychologie des Sports" (All-Union Conference in U.S.S.R. on Sports Psychology), *Theorie und Praxis der Korperkultur*. Berlin, 7:6, 1958.

83. Roudik, P. A. "Psichologija Sporta" (Sports Psychology), *Psichologiceskaja Nauka v S.S.S.R.* (Psychological Science in the U.S.S.R.). Moscow, II, 1960.

84. Roudik, P. A. "Psichologija Sporta za 50 let" (Sports Psychology During 50 Years), *Voprosy Psichologii* (Psychological Questions), translated and summarized into Czech by V. Hosek, *Teorie a Praxe Telesne Vychovy*. Prague, 6, 59–75, 1967.

85. Schulte, R. W. *Leib und Seele im Sport. Einfuehrung in die Psychologie der Leibesübungen* (Body and Soul in Sports: An Introduction to the Psychology of Physical Exercises). Charlottenburg, 1921.

86. Schulte, R. W. *Eignungs und Leistungsprufung im Sport* (Ability and Performance Testing in Sports). Berlin, 1925.
87. Schulte, R. W. *Leistungssteigerung in Turnen, Spiel und Sport. Grundlinien einer Psychologie* (Increasing Performance in Exercises, Games and Sports Activities, Basic Psychological Outline). Oldenburg, 1927.
88. Singer, Robert N. *Motor Learning and Human Performance.* New York: Macmillan Company, 1968.
89. Sippel, H. *Der Turnunterricht und die Geistige Arbeit des Schulkindes* (Physical Education in Schools and the Mental Work of School Children). Berlin.
90. Sippel, H. *Leibesübungen und die Geistige Arbeit* (Physical Exercises and Mental Activity). Berlin.
91. Skinner, B. F. *The Behavior of Organisms.* New York: Appleton-Century-Crofts, 1938.
92. Slater-Hammel, A. "Measurement of Kinesthetic Perception of Muscular Force with Muscle Potential-Changes." *Res. Quart.,* 1957.
93. Slovenko, R., and Knight, J. A. *Motivations in Play, Games, and Sports.* Springfield, Ill.: Charles C Thomas.
94. Snoody, G. S. *Evidence for Two Opposed Processes in Mental Growth.* Lancaster, Pennsylvania: Science Press, 1935.
95. Steinbach, M. "Sport und Charakter" (Sport and Character), *Sport in Baden.* Karlsruhe, **18**:33, 1964.
96. Stockfelt, T. "Begavnings Analyser av Elitidrottare Simmare" (Analysis of Intelligence of Superior Athletes, Swimmers), *Pedagogiska-Psykologiska Institutionen vid GIH* (Report). Stockholm, 1968.
97. Stockfelt, T. "Performance Under Motivation-Induced Stress." *Forsvarsmedicin,* **3**:2, 60–63, 1967.
98. Stransky, A. *Psychologie Sportu* (Psychology of Sport Activity). Prague: State Physical Education Publisher, 1962.
99. Thorndike, E. L., and Woodworth, R. S. "The Influence of Improvement in One Mental Function upon the Efficiency of Other Functions." *Psych. Rev.,* **8**:247–61, 1901.
100. Thorndike, E. L. "A Note on the Accuracy of Discrimination of Weights and Lengths." *Psych. Rev.,* **16**:340–46, 1909.
101. Triplett, Norman. "The Dynamogenic Factors in Pacemaking and Competition." *Am. J. Psych.,* **9**:507–33, 1897–98.
102. Vanek, M. *Psychologicke Zaklady Telesne Vychovy* (The Psychological Basis of Physical Education). Prague: SPN State Physical Education Publisher, 1963.
103. Wasilewski, E. "Application of the Method of Classifying Questionnaires for Sports Groups." *Proceedings,* First International Congress of Sports Psychology, F. Antonelli (ed.), Rome, 1965.
104. Watson, J. B. "Kinesthetic and Organic Sensations: Their Role in the Reactions of the White Rat to the Maze." *Psych. Monog.,* **8**:33, 49, 1907.

105. Williams, J. F. *Principles of Physical Education.* Philadelphia: W. B. Saunders, 1946.
106. Wischmann, B. *Zum Problem des Mutes in der Korperlichen Erziehung* (The Problem of Courage in Physical Education). Frankfurt/M, 1958.
107. Wohl, A. "Soziale Aspete in der Entwicklung des Massen-Sportes" (Social Aspects in the Development of the Average Sports Activity). *Theorie und Praxie der Korperkultur,* Berlin, 11:7, 1962.
108. Woodworth, R. S. "Accuracy of Voluntary Movement." *Psych. Monog.,* 3:3, 1899.
109. Wundt, W. *Grundlagen der Physiologischen Psychologie* (The Bases of the Physiological Psychology), SPB. Germany, 1911.
110. Yerkes, R. M. "The Mental Life of Monkeys and Apes: A Study of Ideational Behavior." *Behav. Mong.,* 3:12, 1916.
111. Zeigler, E. F. *Philosophical Foundation for Physical, Health and Recreation Education.* Englewood Cliffs, N.J.: Prentice-Hall, 1964.

CHAPTER 2

A Typology of Athletic Activities Based upon Their Psychological Demands

There are a number of typologies of human attributes available. Benjamin Bloom, for example, has attempted to classify cognitive processes, while the factorial work of Fleishman and others has led several writers to attempt to classify motor and perceptual-motor tasks by reference to relationships between performance scores. (1), (2), (3)

The following classification system, started by Kodym (6), is not presently based upon extensive research, but is at this point largely speculative. Essentially the typology outlined below is based partly upon intuitive feelings by the writers, concerning the manner in which athletic activities may be classified with reference to the psychophysical demands required to perform them. At the same time previous attempts to classify sports activities by reference to their psychological characteristics have been consulted. The studies that have provided the primary impetus for the typology on the pages that follow have been carried out by Macak (9), Sledr (11), Vanek and Stransky (12), and Kodym (7).

Within each type of task are listed examples of athletic skills, sports, and similar activities which are typical. At the same time it is apparent that some complex sporting events involve a combination of the attributes required to perform some of the more classifiable athletic competitions arranged within each category. Five examples of broader and more complex athletic categories follow.

1. *Sporting activities involving hand-eye coordinations* constitute the first type of sporting event. Examples of sports whose entire performance falls within this category include archery, shooting, and the like. In addition, specific skills within some of the more complex team sports involve this type of attribute; examples are penalty goal kicking in soccer, free-throw shooting in basketball, and place kicking in American football. Activities within this category are characterized by the need for finite muscular adjustments to visual cues while the visual target is at a single point in space. These types of activities are extremely sensitive to stress from an outside source. Generally tension in these activities grows toward the completion of competition. For example, as a shooter or archer approaches a perfect round, the emotional stress will mount, and his final efforts are less likely to be as accurate as his initial efforts. If the performer achieves success on each trial, then the aspiration level is raised generally as performance continues. There is a tendency for athletes participating in this type of activity to utilize some kind of depressant or other kind of tranquilizing drug prior to and/or during competition. Attention to tasks of this nature is usually required over extensive periods of time.

2. *Sports activities requiring total body coordination and consideration* constitute the second type of sporting event. Activities of this type are those in which the total body moves through space in aesthetically pleasing and precise ways. Included in this event are such activities as free exercise in gymnastics, water ballet, diving, figure skating, ski jumping, and others in which there are points awarded for precision and aesthetic purity. The athlete is working with his own body in space without the necessity of relating his movements to the movements of other people, as is necessary in team sports. The individual's body image is important in these activities with respect to the control and awareness of muscle tonus. Balance, or the correct orientation to gravity, is also important in the correct execution of these activities, while they also involve some degree of artistic creativity on the part of the performer. Correct execution of activities of this nature involves a pleasing arrangement of a series of closely related movements. Usually if a segment of the activity is performed poorly, then the entire impression created by the performer suffers. Psychological characteristics of the performer in these activities usually involve a great deal of pre-task tension, due to the individual's feeling about the possibility of failure and to the inability of the performer to depend upon another individual in his time of stress. Usually activities of this type require the performer to exhibit emotional control for only

a relatively short period of time. If the duration of competition is extended, then the demands upon the performer are usually for short periods of activity interpolated by periods of rest.

3. *Sports activities requiring total mobilization of body energy* constitute the third type of sporting event. Activities in this classification include tasks involving power and/or endurance to varying degrees. Distance running, swimming, and rowing are included in this category. These activities dispel psychological tensions experienced by the athletes, and at the same time a greater amount of pre-task tension is tolerable and may even be helpful in their performances. Athletes may need help in achieving arousal levels high enough to meet the demands of these types of activities, and at times raising the tension level may be practiced by the individual athletes with or without the help of another person. Important to the execution of these tasks is a high level of determination, the ability to ignore pain, and other personality traits denoting persistence and durability. It is usually found that most individuals participating in these types of activities are introverted. They are usually stable emotionally and, in addition, exhibit sound physiological characteristics and good self-control.

An important subcategory of activities within this classification includes activities in which a quick explosive mobilization of energy is necessary. The shot-putter, the sprinter, the high jumper, and the middle guard in American football are examples of athletes within this third category.

4. *Sports activities in which injury or death are imminent* constitute the fourth type of sporting event. Activities within this group include parachute jumping, bob-sledding, race car driving, boxing, downhill skiing, and the like. Participants in these activities often possess explosive personalities, their personality profiles indicating a great deal of toughness and self-discipline. Their reaction times are usually good, both to simple and to complex stimuli, involving both simple and complex responses. These activities are heavily laden with emotional content and are carried out at high speeds. Thus the participants must act quickly but under good control and with sound judgment.

5. *Sports activities involving the anticipation of movements of other people* constitute the fifth type of sporting event. Tasks of this nature involve team sports of various kinds. Tactics are usually important; thus strategical thinking by participants is important. They must react to developing situations and must predict how situations will unfold. Often superior athletic performers in individual skills are not good in team

sports involving these kinds of interactions because they lack the ability to anticipate the movements and reactions of other people with whom they must interact. Individuals in these activities usually possess average or above average I.Q.'s and develop the ability to apply past experiences effectively to current game situations. The individuals participating in tasks of this nature are self-disciplined so that their emotions will not cause them to erupt and to lose self-control. Generally activities of this nature may be divided into three types.

A. Games employing a net, including tennis, volley ball, and table tennis, compose the first type. In these games no direct aggression is possible against one's opponents, but only against the abstract impersonal conditions dictated by the facilities upon which the athlete is playing. Games of this nature require periodic changes of agility, tenacity, and attention, for periods of action are interpolated by periods of attention as the opponents' reactions are observed and evaluated.

B. Games in which direct aggression against one's opponents is possible, including American football, soccer, and ice hockey, compose the second type. Psychological qualities involve mental and physical toughness, speed and endurance, the ability to change the rate of response patterns, and a resistance to pain. In these games there is a specialization of roles, so that a variety of personality types may interact well. The quality of teamwork evidenced may be evaluated sociometrically, and has been by several investigators. The responsibility for winning and/or losing may fall to various players in unequal amounts. They usually evidence tolerance to frustration, useful aggression, and a high sense of social responsibility to others.

C. Games involving parallel play compose the third type. In these games individuals play concurrently or one at a time, with no direct aggression exhibited against their opponents. The players only deal with each other in indirect ways. Examples of activities within this classification include golf, baseball, bowling, and cricket. Teams in these games alternately change roles from offensive actions to defensive actions. The players work against their opponents, but at times they must wait until they may display their aggressions. A high level of tactical strategy is needed, and usually players in these games have average or above average intelligence.

It is apparent that many sports involve a combination of several or all of the above classifications of skill based upon psychological demands. Basketball, for example, involves integration with the movements of others, hand-eye coordinations when shooting, dribbling, and executing free throws, and a total mobilization of body energy at the end of the game. Boxing, as another example, combines subskills which might be classified within each of the five groups. It is inherently dangerous and the objective is often to render an opponent unconscious by inflicting mild temporary cerebral disruption. The endurance demands on the boxer require total energy mobilization; striking and moving require hand-eye coordination of an exact nature, and the blows must be integrated with those of an opponent. Boxing has been described by some observers as an aesthetic sport, particularly when a skillful athlete displays speed of foot and the ability to deliver various combinations of punches.

Despite the rather inexact manner in which the various classifications have been described, they may be helpful in the analysis of various sports and/or various subskills required in different sports relative to the psychological stresses imposed and the psychological requirements demanded of participants. For example, when it is determined that a sport involves skills and qualities within several of the classifications, then it becomes apparent that psychological training of a variety of kinds should be applied to the participants in order to aid them to achieve maximum efficiency.

It is apparent that many types of subtraining procedures should be engaged in by the boxer, for example. He must run for endurance, he must spar for hand-eye skill, and he must engage in frequent practice with unpredictable opponents. Other sports are usually not as complex with regard to the psychological demands placed upon the performer, but the same principles apply. One must analyze the sport and adapt training methods that are revealed in this analysis. These training methods should involve attempts at stress and the attempts to obtain the subsequent adaptations to physical skills and emotional stresses inherent in the activity.

Summary

Although the typology outlined in the previous pages is admittedly speculative, research data are beginning to appear which lend credence to the classifications outlined. Kane (4) has identified through personality tests a "footballer" type, i.e., a Rugby player type, in England. Ogilvie (10) has found a complex of personality traits that seem prevalent in scores of race car drivers, while Kroll (8) has also identified a group of personality traits found in American football players and in wrestlers that indicate a kind of "combative" type. Kroll has also found that there seems to be a type which may correspond to the aesthetic bodily coordination category outlined above, which he derived from inspecting scores obtained from gymnasts and karate performers. Perhaps in future years more definitive categories may be derived after the findings from further research in this area are available.

REFERENCES

1. Bloom, Benjamin E. (ed.). *Taxonomy of Educational Objectives, Handbook I, Cognitive Domain.* New York: David McKay Co., 1963.
2. Fleishman, Edwin A. "Performance Assessment Based on an Empirically Derived Task Taxonomy." *Human Factors,* 9:349–66, 1967.
3. Guilford, H. P. "A System of Psychomotor Abilities." *Am. J. Psych.,* 71: 164–74, 1958.
4. Kane, K. E. "The Discrimination of Sports Types by Means of the I.P.F." Paper read at the British Psychological Society Conference, March 1966.
5. Kodym, M. "Psychologicka Analyza a Charakteristika Sportovni Cinnosti" (The Psychological Analyses and Characteristics of Sports Activity). *Teorie a Praxe Telesne Vychovy,* Prague, 14:12, 1966.
6. Kodym, M. "Psychologicka Typologie Sportu" (The Psychological Typology of Sports Activities). *Teorie a Praxe Telesne Vychovy,* Prague, 14:6, 1966.
7. Kodym, M. "Psychologicke Problemy Indiviualnich Sportu" (Psychological Problems of Individual Sports Activities), *Teoreticke Zaklady Psychologicke Pripravy Sportove* (Theoretical Bases of the Psychological Preparation of Athletes), Miroslav Vanek (ed.). Prague: Czechoslovakian Committee of Physical Education, 1967, No. 2/13.
8. Kroll, Walter, and Crenshaw, William. "Multivariate Personality Profile Analysis of Four Athletic Groups." Paper read at the Second International Congress of Sports Psychology, Washington, D.C., 1968.
9. Macak, I. "Psychologicka Charakteristika Kopane, Odbijene, Ledniho Mokeje" (Psychological Characteristics of Soccer, Volleyball, Ice Hockey) in I. Macak, *Psychologia Sportu* (Psychology of Sport), Bratislava: Sportove Vydavatelstvo, 1962.
10. Ogilvie, Bruce E. "Psychological Consistencies Within the Personality of High Level Competitors." *J. Am. Med. Assoc.,* Special Olympic Year Edition, September–October 1968.

11. Sledr, J. "Psychologicke Problemy Kolektivnich Sportu" (Psychological Problems of Group Sports Activities), *Teoreticke Zaklady Psychologicke Pripravy Sportove* (Theoretical Bases of the Psychological Preparation of Athletes), Miroslav Vanek (ed.). Prague: Czechoslovakian Committee of Physical Education, 1967, No. 2/13.
12. Vanek, M., and Stransky, A. "Psychological Characteristics of Several Individual and Group Sports Activities," *Encyklopedie Telesne Vychovy a Sportu* (Encyclopedia of Physical Education and Sports, K. Hala and F. Pavek (eds.). Prague: Czechoslovakian Physical Education Publisher, 1964.

II

EVALUATION
OF THE
SUPERIOR ATHLETE

A NUMBER of tools and approaches have been utilized over the years to assess the attributes of outstanding athletes. At times they have been scrutinized on the playing field and in more structured field tests that are similar to those outlined in *The Assessment of Men* (Ch. 3, 14). In addition, standard personality and sociometric scales from a number of countries have been employed to evaluate superior sports performances. A third primary way in which athletes have been studied is through the use of standard laboratory tests of performance. Within the latter category, tests of both simple and complex reaction time, steadiness measures, and various coordination tests involving bodily integrations, as well as tasks involving hand-eye coordinations, have been employed.

It is possible to trace historical trends in the use of these kinds of testing instruments. Initially, during the 1920's and the 1930's, an athlete or group of athletes was often brought to the psychologist's laboratory and subjected to various performance tests. After a period of time, however, it was realized that the measures obtained did little to predict athletic success in the complex athletic contests in which a number of motivational, emotional, as well as psychomotor variables impinged upon performance.

Thus within more recent years a variety of interesting field tests have been employed. These tests have been of two kinds. At times athletes have been filmed and/or observed in actual athletic contests. They have been rated

49

concerning the aggressiveness they demonstrated, the appropriateness of their responses in given tactical situations, as well as in other obvious and subtle traits they evidenced. A second kind of field test has been of a more contrived nature. For example, a group of athletes may be subjected to a course containing unknown and unfamiliar obstacles. Observers placed near each of the obstacles may then rate the aggressiveness, will power, and/or the efficiency with which individual sportsmen, as well as groups in various sports, negotiate the situations with which they are suddenly confronted.

The material which follows has been organized into several chapters. Initially the historical trends in measurement and evaluation of the athlete are discussed. Following this first section, discussions of the various methods of evaluating athletic competency are presented, including personality assessments, measurement of physical attributes, evaluation of game performances, as well as the manner in which various structured field tests are employed.

This section concludes with an evaluation of these assessment tools, together with implications for further research and for refinement of the evaluative devices and techniques which have been employed in the ways described.

CHAPTER 3

Personality Assessment

Personality assessments of superior athletes have been carried out for the past ten years. These evaluations have had several purposes. Some of them were originally formulated to evaluate psychiatric patients and were not well suited to the normal and superior human subject. For example, the Knobloch Neurotic Scale was sometimes employed. (5) At times these first measures were only subjective self-analyses of the athlete's personal life, general feelings about performance, his family constitution, and the like. After using tools of this type for several years, it was found that the information they provided was difficult to evaluate and to apply in the psychological training of the athlete.

By the 1960's, sophisticated personality scales were starting to be employed. (8) These were of several types and were obtained from several sources throughout the world. (19) For example, the Eysenck Personality Inventory was used by some sport psychologists. (7) The attributes evaluated on the Eysenck scale may be ranged on several scales, including stability-instability, introversion-extroversion, and from these a general evaluation of an athlete's temperament may be made. In addition, from the Eysenck scale one may obtain a lie score.

The Raven Picture (nonverbal) I.Q. test also was incorporated into many of the batteries employed. (16) This test was used because the diverse cultural backgrounds of the various athletes would have made a verbal test of I.Q., usually employed with adults, invalid. The Raven test is reasonably well standardized, but is not valid in the measurement of I.Q.'s above 120.

Taylor's test of manifest anxiety is also employed by many. (20) This rather direct measure of what has been termed "Manifest Anxiety" (the anxiety of an individual which he will admit to via questionnaire) contains statements to which the respondent answers yes or no. Examples of the questions include "Do you have difficulty sleeping at night? _____," "Are you easily upset? _____." This test was employed extensively to measure changes in anxiety levels of superior athletes prior to, during, and following competition. Members of several of the teams competing in the Mexico City Olympics were evaluated using this measure of general fear or foreboding.

The Cattell test of sixteen personality factors (2), (3) has also been used extensively. The three forms of this test purport to evaluate introversion, extroversion, intelligence, emotional stability (frustration tolerance), dominance-submission, surgency-passivity, self-control–lack of self-control, adventurous-conservative, sensitive-tough, realistic, paranoid-adaptable, imaginative-practical, and so on.

The Cattell has also been used to plot the profiles of individual athletes, and to facilitate the comparison of their profiles to group means of average populations. Groups of athletes in various sports were also contrasted using the Cattell. Guidelines for the psychological training of an individual athlete are often obtained from inspection of the Cattell scores. Weaknesses and strong points within an athlete's personality are thus identifiable, and psychotherapeutic measures may be undertaken if necessary.

The data from the Cattell is also used to evaluate groups of athletes engaging in various sports. In various dual sports (i.e., double sculls), proper matching of personality types is sometimes accomplished using the trait scores from the Cattell.

Other scales employed by American and English researchers during the years are the Edwards Personal Preference Schedule (4), the Maudsley Psychological Inventory, and the Minnesota Multiphasic Personality Inventory. Investigations by Booth, La Place, and Slusher, for example, using the MMPI, have explored personality trait differences between athletes and nonathletes, and between superior performers and less capable sportsmen. (1), (11), (17)

A personality and interest test formulated by the German researchers, Mittenecker and Toman, is also employed to assess athletes. (18) This latter measure was used more in a clinical than in an experimental context to identify possible psychotic and neurotic problems among athletes, including paranoid and schizoid tendencies, and the like. Other factors evaluated include the degree of self-criticism, social ability, introversion, neurotic symptoms, maniac symptoms, depressive symptoms, paranoid symptoms, and physiological stability that the athlete may evidence.

Evaluation of the tests outlined above is sometimes carried out by comparing the data obtained on individual athletes with their coaches' assessments of their athletes' personality trait structures.

Data obtained by physicians are also compared with data obtained from the personality assessments and psychomotor tests to further validate the latter measures. For example, physicians' ratings of groups of athletes from best to least proficient corresponded closely (in a given day) to the same ratings given the same group of athletes by both the psychologists and by their coaches.

Several important considerations were usually followed when administering batteries of personality measures to athletes. First, for example, the administration of personality measures to athletes was often carried out within a reasonably short time interval. Concentration was found to be better on shorter tests. Athletes enjoy athletics, not sitting and filling out questionnaires. Both authors have obtained responses that reflect frustration and hostility from athletes whose activity has been interfered with by answering questionnaires. More than two sessions of about two hours in duration will usually prove oppressive to athletes. The entire Minnesota Multiphasic Personality Inventory, for example, takes too long to administer, thus making its inclusion questionable in a battery for the evaluation of athletes. (6)

Secondly, the athlete should be afforded the opportunity to review the data obtained about him. He should be made to feel that he will benefit directly from the measures obtained. The data should be used as a basis for counseling the athlete.

The information should be collected in surroundings familiar to the athlete. The psychologist should, if possible, go to the athlete, rather than requiring that he come to the psychological laboratory. Athletes, like most people, do not regard themselves as laboratory animals. Thus the laboratory is often a poor environment in which to collect reliable data from athletes.

The use of several types of tests to evaluate the same personality trait was found to be helpful because athletes are often expansive and exhibitionistic when answering questions on personality scales. Thus the various tests provide verification of the responses of the athletes taking them.

In addition to the standardized personality tests described, Hosek has evolved a self-rating scale that supplies additional information from the athletes themselves. (9) The questions on the rating scale were initially obtained from open-ended questionnaires that were administered. This type of self-opinion test may contain questions concerning the athlete's feelings about his last competitive performance, ability to relax and to sleep at night, whether his appetite is good, his general emotional outlook, whether he is depressed or elated, his feelings about the training camp, and his feelings about the group with whom he is training, including his coach, whether he is easily fatigued or not, the leisure-time activities he participates in, the recreational pursuits he would like to engage in, his sexual life, and occurrences during the day of the interview that made the athlete happy or discontented.

The questions on this type of self-interview are usually constructed so that they provide a series of checks and balances on each other. Thus inconsistencies in the athlete's responses to such a self-interview provide important clues to the psychologist's evaluation of his emotional welfare.

This self-interview is often repeated at regular intervals, sometimes as frequently as every second or third day. In this manner the dynamic cyclic changes in the athlete's outlook on himself, his training, and his total social and emotional welfare may be monitored.

In addition to the momentary feelings an athlete evidences on the self-interview, he is often required to write a brief autobiography, including the characteristics of his family upbringing, the nature of the family unit, as well as other pertinent information.

Sociometric measures are also employed to determine the group and individual feelings among sports teams. The Moreno "guess who" type of sociometric test is often employed. (13) For example, the athlete is asked to assess a member of a team who reacts to him in various ways, and at the same time to assess how he feels about the various members of the team. There are thirty-three questions of each type, one group of questions evaluating how the athlete feels about members of the team, and the other thirty-three evaluating how the athlete thinks the group feels about him.

The social dimensions revealed on this type of social assessment, such as dominance, submission, aggression, friendships, and social distance, when graphed, provide a reasonably complete picture of the social behavior expected in the group, as well as more subtle social dynamics of the situation in which the team functions. The Leary test (12) is also used to obtain a personality profile based upon an athlete's self-image, as well as his feelings about an individual with whom he is associating closely, i.e., his doubles partner in tennis. Some of the twelve attributes assessed on this test include introversion-extroversion, impulsivity-stability, leadership-followership, sociability-unsociability, rigid-flexible, and the like. The results of this test, of course, may be compared to the scores of the other personality tests described, if several tests of this nature are placed in a battery to which athletes are exposed. Marked discrepancies indicate that perhaps one of the tests may need review, or that perhaps the athlete is being too protective and thus becomes inconsistent in his responses to the questions posed. If correct interpretation of the data is obtained from the Leary test, one is able to ascertain the discrepancy an individual feels between his own self-rating and his idealized self-rating, as well as the difference perceived between his own personality trait structure and that of another individual in close proximity on the sports team.

Depending upon the country of Europe examined, one will find various emphases placed upon these types of tests. The Russians and Bulgarians depend upon physiological measures, rather than upon paper-and-pencil assessments of personality. The behavioral scientists in Poland have developed a reasonably sophisticated battery of sociometric tests. In the Democratic Republic of Germany (East Germany) a series of rating scales to be used by coaches have been constructed. These scales are used by the coaches to rate the emotional behavior, tactical proficiency in group games, technical proficiency, frustration level in losing, and other attributes of their players prior to, during, and following athletic competition.

The measures of personality assessment used in the various countries have many purposes, including the following:

1. They are used to select individuals who may be expected to exhibit proficiency in future years. This is carried out in countries in which there are relatively few athletes from which to choose.

2. The data obtained is also used to identify "problem athletes," as well as to devise effective means for dealing with the psychological

makeup of athletes who display no special personality and/or emotional problems.

3. The personality measures obtained from groups of athletes aid in defining the exact parameters of various types of sports teams. The typical personality structure of, for example, the gymnast, the distance runner, and the football player may be demonstrated with the use of personality and sociometric measures of the types described.

4. The personality trait scores may be compared to data collected on the same athletes by the physiologist, the physician, as well as to psychomotor tests administered by the experimental psychologist. Clusters of scores indicative of groups of stable psychological-physiological-sociological traits may thus be obtained through the use of factor analytic techniques.

5. With continued investigations, and particularly with the standardization of measurement techniques within various countries, it will become possible to engage in comparisons of athletes within various cultures and between various socioeconomic groups within the same country. Comparison of personalities of athletes within various climatic zones in the world may also be undertaken when methodologies become more highly standardized.

6. With continued investigations of the personality of athletes, a valid theoretical framework should emerge within which the personality of the sportsman may be considered.

It is helpful to utilize tests which may be administered to groups of athletes. It is virtually impossible to obtain data from large numbers of athletes if an investigator must give a test on a one-to-one basis. And it is often true that unless large groups of athletes are surveyed, the results of the investigation are of little validity. One of the major drawbacks in previous investigations of the personalities of athletes is that extremely small samples have been used.

In general, the tests outlined may be administered within the indicated time intervals:

> Cattell Sixteen Item: 60–80 minutes
> Eysenck Personality Inventory: 8–10 minutes
> Taylor's Manifest Anxiety Test: 8–10 minutes
> Raven's Intelligence Test: 25–30 minutes
> Guess-Who Sociometric Test: 35–40 minutes

Leary's Test: 40–50 minutes
Self-rating Scale: 15–20 minutes

Thus it is possible to administer the above tests with two testing sessions, each lasting about two hours.

It appears more helpful if a reasonably extensive and comprehensive battery of tests is administered rather than a single test or two. The differences in the findings of investigators attempting to differentiate personality differences between athletes and nonathletes is probably due to the fact that only one measure of personality was used and at the same time only a very few subjects were employed in such investigations.

Further confusion occurs when attempting to interpret the findings of studies of the personality dynamics of athletes from various cultures because the term "athlete" is not clearly defined.

Future progress in the evaluation of the personality trait structure of athletes should occur if more standardized measures are used. A standard definition of an "athlete" acceptable to all should be arrived at. If a comprehensive battery of personality, sociometric, self-reporting techniques and projective measures is agreed upon by researchers from various countries, fruitful intercultural comparisons may be carried out.

Most of the personality measures outlined on these pages were not specifically constructed for the evaluation of athletes, but rather are standard personality tests utilized in a number of clinical and experimental contexts. It is believed that more valid results will be obtained when personality measures specifically designed to evaluate athletes are developed. Future batteries should have tests at several levels, including a basic and comprehensive personality measure. In addition, more specific measures evaluating athletes competing in specific events and in various positions in team sports should be utilized. Additionally, tests evaluating the emotional states within specific situations might also be constructed, i.e., to assess feelings when losing and after winning.

REFERENCES

1. Booth, E. G. "Personality Traits of Athletes Measured by the MMPI." *Res. Quart.*, 29:127–38, 1958.

58   EVALUATION OF THE SUPERIOR ATHLETE

2. Cattell, R. B., and Eber, H. W. *Handbook for the Sixteen Personality Factor Questionnaire*. Illinois: IPAT, 1957.
3. Cattell, R. B. *The Scientific Analysis of Personality*. New York: Penguin Books, 1965.
4. Edwards, A. L. "Edwards Personal Preference Schedule," Manual. New York: Psychological Corporation, 1954, p. 36.
5. Engelsmann, F. "Dotaznikove Metody a Jejich Diagnosticke Pouziti (The Questionnaire Method and Its Use in Evaluation), *Csl. Psychologie* (Czechoslovakian Psychology), 4, 1960.
6. Engelsmann, F. "Nase zkvsenosti S Minesotskym Dotaznikem" (Experiences with the MMPI), *Csl. Psychologie* (Czechoslovakian Psychology), 3, 1959.
7. Eysenck, H. J. *Manual of the Maudsley Personality Inventory*. ULP, 1959.
8. Hall, C. S., and Lindzey, G. *Theories of Personality*. New York: John Wiley and Sons, 1957.
9. Hosek, V., and Vanek, M. "Construction and Application of a Specific Rating Scale for the Evaluation of Actual Psychical States of the Athlete." Paper read at the Second International Congress of Sports Psychology, Washington, D.C., 1968.
10. Kane, J. E., and Warburton, F. W. "Personality Relates to Sports and Physical Ability," in *Readings in Physical Education*. London: The Physical Education Association, 1966, Chapter 4.
11. La Place, J. P. "Personality and Its Relationship to Success in Professional Football." *Res. Quart.*, 25:313–19, 1954.
12. Leary, T. F. *Interpersonal Diagnosis of Personality, A Functional Theory and Methodology for Personality Evaluation*. New York: Ronald Press, 1957.
13. Moreno, J. L., and Jennings, H. H. "Statistics and Social Configurations." *Sociometry*, 1:239–54, 1938.
14. O.S.S. (Office of Strategic Services). *The Assessment of Men*. New York: Holt, Rinehart, 1948.
15. Petrak, B. *Sociologie v Telesne Kultur* (Sociology in Physical Culture). Prague: State Pedagogical Publisher, 1967.
16. Raven, J. C. *Guide to Using Progressive Matrices*. London: H. K. Lewis, 1950.
17. Slusher, H. S. "Personality and Intelligence Characteristics of Selected High School Athletes and Non-Athletes." *Res. Quart.*, 35:539–45, December 1964.
18. Stransky, A., and Hoskovec, J. "Uziti Psychologickych Diagnostickych Metod v Telesne Vychove a Sportu" (The Use of Psychological Diagnostic Methods in Physical Education and Sport). *Teorie a Praxe Telesne Vychovy a Sportu*, Prague, 11, 1962.
19. Tardy, V. *Psychologie Osobnosti* (The Psychology of Personality). Prague: State Pedagogical Publisher, 1964.
20. Taylor, J. A. "A Personality Scale of Manifest Anxiety." *J. Abnorm. Soc. Psychol.*, 5:23–32, 1953.

CHAPTER 4

Assessing the Athlete Through Field Tests

Initial attempts to predict athletic performance in competition through data collected in the research laboratory were not generally successful. For example, it was usually found that measures of simple reaction times were not indicative of the quickness with which an athlete could make the correct decisions in complicated games. Similarly, measures of the strength of individual muscle groups were often not helpful in predicting how successful an athlete would be in using his power in various weight events and in track-and-field competitions.

Sports psychologists in Europe, therefore, began to cast about for better ways of evaluating the superior athlete. (17) Their searches led to two general methodologies. In one methodology the athlete was measured while actually engaged in individual and in team competition. For example, observers were sometimes assigned to observe a single athlete during an entire athletic contest, and to rate his aggressiveness, his competence in the execution of strategic moves when confronted with changing game conditions, his speed and quickness, and his reactions to frustration. (4) At other times films were taken of individual athletes during game conditions and, after replaying them for extensive periods of time, they were rated in a similar way. (2)

Structured field tests were contrived through which to assess the various qualities believed important in athletic competitions. For example, a group of athletes representing various sports might be placed on a course through the forest containing obstacles with which they were unfamiliar.

59

Observers stationed near each of these obstacles, which might consist of a water jump, a pit to swing over, walls to climb, and so on, would rate the manner in which each athlete negotiated the various problems. For example, it would be noted whether the athlete hesitated when confronted with a particularly difficult wall to ascend or whether he unhesitatingly vaulted it. (25) Individual characteristics were noted by using this type of test as well as group characteristics typical of the performers in several common sports. At times, however, the nature of the obstacle might favor a particular kind of athlete. For example, the gymnast would be less likely to encounter problems in negotiating high obstacles than would the track athlete and the soccer player who, in turn, would be more capable when negotiating jumps and low hurdles and when maintaining speed and competence should the course become long and their endurance become taxed.

Figure 1. Experiments of courage have taken many forms. In the one shown, the athlete is being observed as he traverses one of a series of obstacles. He has had no previous knowledge of the nature of the obstacle course he has just entered, nor does he know that he is being observed as he attempts to negotiate each obstacle. The experimenters record the speed with which he traverses each obstacle, the presence of reactions denoting anxiety, as well as the general "style" he may exhibit during the running of the course. In general it is usually found that "courage" exhibited is related to the athlete's performance specialty. For example, gymnasts go over obstacles requiring gymnastic ability with little trouble, long jumpers negotiate the water jumps well.

Several other types of field tests were utilized by sports psychologists. (5) Russian sports psychologists (23), (19) and physiologists (14) have theorized that various perceptual discriminations which athletes make become more acute with continued exposure to practice and competition. It has been assumed that the athlete's kinesthetic, visual, and auditory discriminations, relative to the sensory input inherent in the athletic competition, become more acute. Muscular and cardiovascular changes were assumed to be taking place also. For example, in middle-distance and long-distance running it has been proposed that an athlete's time sense becomes heightened with exposure to running conditions. (21) Pursuing this theory, several experimenters have studied this discrimination of time among experienced and inexperienced runners. As might be expected, the experienced runners demonstrated the ability to run 400-, 800-, and 1,500-meter races within tenths of a second of the times suggested before the races, while the less experienced runners were able to approach the times given to them only within very broad ranges and usually missed the times set for them by several seconds. (31) Such experiments demonstrate the remarkable acquisition of a rather exact time sense among athletes who are continually exposed to training and competition.

The information from these experiments has been utilized by track coaches in Russia when preparing track athletes for competition. Accompanying the usual training to enhance the cardiovascular improvement necessary in distance running has been a parallel effort to make the runners aware of the exact times they are talking to traverse a given distance. Thus training in time sense accompanies training for endurance and running speed.

Further investigations in Russia and Czechoslovakia (13) relating the stability of the time sense to various personality trait scores have revealed that athletes who are subject to a great amount of emotional stress prior to and during competition frequently experience difficulty when judging the pace of their efforts. The time sense thus is likely to be interfered with when the athlete is under duress and/or when emotionally unstable athletes enter competitions.

Several researchers have been interested in the manner in which the ball is perceived by soccer players, volleyball players, and athletes interested in gaining proficiency in similar sports. (14) This ball sense is actually made up of the accuracy with which an individual may perceive a ball's shape, size, weight, surface conditions, such as wetness or dryness, and similar qualities. In laboratory tests it has been found that, when blindfolded, the better athletes in these ball-handling sports are more accurate in the manner in which they can discriminate between balls of various weights, sizes, and degrees of surface conditions. These tests have been carried out using blindfolded soccer players, in which the discriminations had to be made with the feet; and with volleyball players, in which the discriminations of several balls had to be made by using the hands. At times the athletes have been asked to determine which of several balls are most like the standard ball used in their sport.

Figure 2. The "ball sense" of soccer players is sometimes scored by determining how quickly and accurately they can discriminate between a standard soccer ball and other balls differing slightly in size, shape, texture, and/or weight. The athletes are blindfolded and use their feet to test the soccer balls, as shown in the drawing.

Training in the ball sense has been carried out in sports which utilize balls. For example, balls of various weights, sizes, and degrees of hardness are often used in practice in the gymnasium or on the athletic field. It is believed that through these methods a heightened "ball sense" is achieved by players manipulating spheres with their hands and/or their feet.

Basketball players have been given dark glasses to wear in practice in order to block out some of the visual cues they usually depend upon. It is felt that through this means the ball sense of basketball players may be heightened.

Similar to the findings regarding the loss of time sense, it has been found that athletes tend to become less able to make the discriminations which depend upon their ball sense under the stress of competition. It has also been found that athletes who are less stable emotionally have more difficulty sensing the nature of the ball which they are manipulating with their hands and/or their feet.

Figure 3. Studies of athletes' "ball sense" are carried out by asking the blindfolded subject to make fine discriminations between the weights, sizes, and shapes of balls similar to and identical with those used in his own sport. The speed as well as the accuracy of these judgments are recorded. It is usually found that the better players possess a more highly refined "ball sense" than do the less able players.

Interesting experiments were carried out with athletes in a number of sports in which balance attributes were investigated. (3), (22) Specifically, these studies dealt with the role of various components of the human action system which might have an influence on good balance. In some studies the athlete's hearing was blocked while he attempted to perform components of the skill involved in his sport. In other research peripheral vision was eliminated with glasses. In still other investigations central vision was blocked in the same manner. (27) Some subjects had collars placed on their necks to immobilize head movements, which play a role in the maintenance of a proper orientation to gravity, during both static and dynamic balance activities. Studied using this technique was the manner in which various components of the human action system influenced an athlete's performance in balance tasks and various sports. It was found that elimination of central or peripheral vision was most disruptive of dynamic balance in basketball performance; both kinesthetic cues as well as visual information seemed important to the gymnastic performer; and rowers were not affected by the elimination of peripheral or central vision, but their rhythm was upset with the elimination of auditory cues. On the other hand, divers and figure skaters were markedly affected by removing movement cues emanating from the neck, as well as by the obliteration of either peripheral or central vision even when asked to perform relatively simple tasks, such as jumping from a diving board from a standing position.

The experimenters theorized that in a given athletic activity there is one most important component of the sensory apparatus influential on good performance. It was hoped by these experiments to determine which component—hearing, kinesthesis, vision, or tactual sensation—was most important in each sport in order to afford coaches guidelines for more effective training.

Other studies of balance compared scores obtained from athletes in a number of sports, using a stabilometer. This activity involved an athlete's attempt to stand on an unstable platform and keep it level. It was found that the gymnasts and weight lifters usually performed best in this type of activity.

As might be expected, sensory acuity within a number of modalities was often found to be blunted under the stress of actual competition or of imminent competition, as well as in athletes whose personality profiles indicated the presence of disruptive psychological states.

Russian sport psychologists have performed a number of interesting experiments which focused upon the memory of athletes. Some of these experiments were carried out with the slalom skiers. (12) The participants were asked to first walk up a hill containing the gates to be traversed, and then at the top of the hill they were asked to diagram the course they had just observed. Analysis of the drawings following competition revealed that the best performers also performed best in the memory tasks assigned to them prior to descending the hill. Participants in water slalom were also involved in these studies.

The results of experiments of this nature have suggested that specific memory training be given to athletes participating in events in which memory is important. (30) Serial memory tasks involving the imitation of a number of movements in correct order appear in the training regimes of superior athletes, as well as in the programs for the less adept individuals.

Similar to these experiments in simple serial memory ability, other experiments involved athletes who were asked to describe the tactics they would employ when later attempting to traverse a simple downhill skiing course. (11) Analyses of these responses have also been compared to the actual performance of the competitors, revealing that good tacticians are generally the more rapid performers.

A number of studies of complex reaction time have been carried out by sports psychologists in Czechoslovakia, Russia, Bulgaria, and Poland. Initially the skiers participated in experiments in which their reaction time to simple and to complex stimuli were obtained. These scholars also investigated reaction time involving complex hand-arm responses to light cues.

After these data had been obtained, the subjects were filmed reacting to the same kinds of light cues while skiing. (6) A given configuration of light cues, for example, indicated a left turn, another indicated a right turn, and a third was the signal to proceed straight ahead. The skiers' reactions were also clocked as they passed the gates along a course and as they saw and reacted to the light cues.

The findings indicated that while one could not differentiate between proficient and inexperienced skiers by analyzing the data collected in the laboratory, significant differences between the two groups were obtained in the field studies of complex reaction time. It was concluded that each sport activity involves reactions to highly specific cues and that laboratory training in quickness will probably not transfer to the sport itself.

It should be pointed out, however, that in this particular experiment the reactions in the laboratory involved only arm-hand movements, while those in the field involved total body movement. Thus it is difficult to separate the influence of the change in the response characteristics from the fact that the subjects were placed on skis.

Experiments involving a combination of reaction time and movement speed were also carried out within the laboratory, using handball, soccer, and basketball players. (26) The subjects in the three sports (both proficient and inexperienced performers) were placed in front of an apparatus

Figure 4. Various field tests of complex reaction time were devised after it was found that laboratory data evaluating both simple and complex reaction time were not predictive of athletes' success in sports. In the experiment illustrated, the skier is required to quickly pass through one of the gates in response to light cues which are flashed as he breaks the electronic eye. The accuracy of his decision and the speed with which he makes it are determined by filming the experiment via high-speed movie cameras.

containing three buttons. They were required to press a specified button when one of three balls placed in front of them descended. The subjects had to move their total body six feet in order to touch the switches.

Upon reviewing the data obtained under the laboratory conditions, the findings of these studies revealed that there were significant differences between the athletes who were proficient in the sport and those who were not. The tasks involving a combination of reaction time, or movement speed of the total body to a reasonably complex stimulus array, were predictive of good sports performance; however, tests of simple reaction time were not.

Further studies which required more complex reactions to lights and to moving balls as cues produced findings which suggested that the scores differed even among high-level performers in various ball games. These latter experiments required the subject to stand on a switch and react by first running and turning off a light and then by turning and throwing a ball into another target. Thus reaction time and complex movement responses could be measured separately. The target to which the subject was required to throw the ball was changed from trial to trial, and was designated by a light on the target box.

This latter experiment also involved judgment time as an important variable. Correlations between judgment time and tactics employed by the performers as rated through observations were reasonably high, thus demonstrating that the more complex the experimental arrangements within the laboratory, the more likely they are to predict performance on the athletic field. Thus experiments in which complex judgments are required within the laboratory are more likely to predict the quality of complex judgments encountered under competitive conditions.

The experiments reviewed, together with other studies carried out in Russia during the last several years, have pointed to a sequence of reaction time–judgment time experiments which may be arranged in order of difficulty. (24) The least difficult are simple reaction time studies within the laboratory; next would be complex reaction time studies within the laboratory, including reactions to complex stimulus displays and/or involving complex responses; next are experiments in which more complex judgments are called for in various field experiments, including the studies of skiers previously discussed. The most difficult type of experiment involves the measurement of judgment time under complicated game conditions, or under laboratory conditions, in which several types of judgments must be made; the latter studies would include reactions to light cues by running to the proper light, retrieving a ball and then throwing to one or several targets, which again may be designated by a second light cue.

Thus in the training processes it has been hypothesized that the athlete gains attributes involving reaction time, movement speed, and judgment time which become increasingly specific to the sport in which he is engaged. While in many cases these proper reactions are developed naturally while participating in sports of various kinds, it also becomes the responsibility of the coach to delineate just what responses are desired in each sport and to give an athlete specific training to accelerate as much as possible the process of acquisition of correct responses.

Thus several sports psychologists in Europe are in the process of developing batteries of tests ranging from simple to complex tasks, which exactly delineate the types of responses needed within specific sports. These tests, administered both in the laboratory and in the field, should add to knowledge of coaching methodologies as well as to basic understanding of the reactions and responses of superior performers under the stresses of competition.

An example of the more complex problems for studying athletes now being devised by psychologists is a test in which the subject is quickly presented via a tachistoscope with various situations he may meet within a given sport. (15) Thus, given a complex visual picture of a sports situation, the athlete is required to think and to write out replies to a questionnaire rather than to perform any reactions.

Psychologists in Czechoslovakia, East Germany, and Poland have developed sets of twenty or more pictures of situations in such sports as volleyball, soccer, ice hockey, and similar sports. (34) Each picture contains more than one player, a ball or puck, and depicts the players in action.

These pictures are presented to individual athletes only for a fraction of a second, sometimes for as short an interval as one tenth of a second. The athlete is then asked to make several kinds of judgments concerning what he has just seen, including:

1. What he has seen: how many players, where they are going, where the ball is, and so on.

2. What has transpired before, based upon his current impressions gained from the quick inspection of the picture: where the players come from, who just passed the ball.

3. What will happen next: where the players are going, where the ball is traveling, who will get the ball next.

And most important

4. What he should do when confronted with the situation depicted: what offensive or defensive moves he should make, should he attempt to contact the ball or to contact a man.

These kinds of assessments have been found to be helpful in evaluating sportsmen. (16) The validation has been carried out by asking coaches to rate the general competency of players in game situations and to compare their rating to the scores obtained from the tachistoscopic tests described. Further refinements of these tests and the resultant questionnaires should prove even more helpful in the assessment and in the training of superior

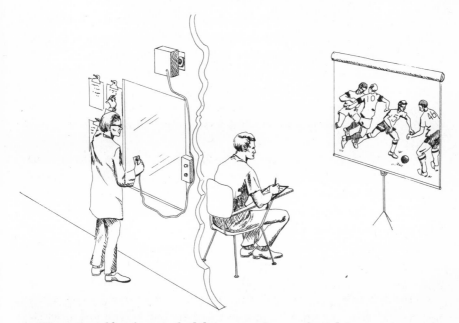

Figure 5. Athletes' tactical abilities are often evaluated in experiments in which pictures of sports interactions are quickly flashed as shown. After the picture is no longer present, the athlete must determine what players were present, where the ball was, what the athletes were doing, what they probably will do next, what they probably did just prior to the picture, and what he would do in the situation. It is usually found that better tacticians in the field are also those who do best in this type of experiment. These techniques have also been used to train tactical abilities in team-sport athletes. Picture series for soccer, ice hockey, and basketball have been employed in this manner.

athletes in an even greater variety of sports in the English-speaking countries and in Central and Eastern Europe.

It has been found that it is not possible to predict the poor and superior athletes from experiments in which abstract figures are presented in the manner described above. Rather the pictures must be of concrete realistic situations to which the athlete has been exposed in training and to which he will be exposed in the future in order for valid conclusions to be drawn. Thus the findings of these experiments further suggest that only when the laboratory situations closely approximate the real competitive situations will helpful data emerge.

A number of studies have also explored what has been termed the influence of ideomotor practice. (29), (28) This corresponds in general to some of the research in what has been called, within the English-American psychological literature, mental practice, or conceptualizing. This mental practice has been instituted by some coaches of gymnastics, of diving, and of track-and-field events within their athletes' practice regimes. Many athletes both in the English-speaking countries and throughout the world engage in some kind of "thinking through their routine" just prior to performing free exercise or springing off a diving board.

Controlled experiments both in Czechoslovakia and in Russia have been carried out exploring the effect of this type of ideomotor practice upon superior athletes. (18) One investigation involved fifteen subjects in an experimental group and fifteen control subjects, all of whom were triple jumpers. (9)

The experimental group members were required to memorize the exact verbal formula describing the numerous complex actions taking place during the triple jump, such as "lift the right arm, take a step with the left foot, and so on." After they had memorized these directions, they were required to repeat them to themselves just prior to falling asleep and, if possible, to picture the actions in their minds while this kind of internal verbalizing was taking place. This practice was continued for a period of six months. At the end of this time there was a difference reported in triple-jump performance in favor of the experimental group amounting to thirty centimeters. The final testing was carried out under competitive conditions. However, as is true of many studies carried out within these countries, statistical procedures acceptable to behavioral scientists in America were not applied to the data. Thus it is difficult to interpret the gain in the reported mean score.

This type of ideomotor practice prior to competing is often encouraged by sports psychologists in order to distract the athlete from his personal pre-task tensions and to encourage him to move outside himself and to worry about the task rather than about his own internalized fears. (1), (20) A recent study in the United States found that mental practice during the initial stages of learning a motor skill was as effective as physical practice during the same period of time. It is believed that, with refined methodologies and the applications of mental practice studied as possibly effective of a variety of sports skill and subskills, the worth of mental practice or ideomotor practice may be more fully exploited.

An interesting series of experiments exploring the nature of courage in athletes in a number of sports was carried out in Czechoslovakia in the 1950's. (32) Subjects were obtained from several groups of participants in activities which purportedly require courage, including motorcycle race drivers, ski jumpers, downhill skiers, parachute jumpers, and gymnasts. A group of experienced divers was used as a control, since the tasks in which courage was to be tested consisted of both diving and jumping from a three-meter diving board. The measures of courage obtained included the time needed for each performer to make the decision to jump, which was timed from a starting signal to the time the individual left the board, as well as an assessment of fear reactions in facial as well as in bodily gestures and postures. The latter measures were assessed by two observers on a three-point scale, consisting of "no fear," "moderate fear," and "marked fear," from films taken of each subject while on the diving board. The subjects were also asked to make the same judgments of their own fear following both dives. About 12 per cent of the subjects refused to dive head first, while all the subjects jumped feet first.

Another interesting measure was taken of the subject's ability to make perceptual judgments under the stress imposed. Numbers ranging from one to nine were placed adjacent to the pool, and one was exposed as the subject left the board. Following each dive, the subject was asked to report the number he saw during his dive.

The most important finding was that courage seems to be specific to the sport involved. The trained divers, as would be expected, evidenced no fear, reported that they were not fearful, and reported the number seen during the dive accurately. The performers in the other "courageous" activities, however, evidenced marked fear, which was revealed in the amount of time they needed to execute the jump, in facial and bodily postures they assumed, and in the inability to perceive the numbers after leaving the board. This phenomenon of perceptual disturbance under stressful conditions is documented with frequency in the experimental literature.

In general, the performers of activities in which jumping was a component, such as ski jumpers and parachutists, evidenced slightly less fear than did the performers of activities in which they are not usually free from the ground, such as downhill skiers and motorcycle race drivers. However, the amount of fear to which all the subjects admitted in the questionnaire they filled out was significantly less than the amount of

Figure 6. Courage has been evaluated by requiring athletes to jump and dive from high diving boards. Anxiety reactions are filmed, and response delays are timed. In general, as might be expected, trained divers perform best, while athletes from sports that require them to be in the air (e.g., parachuting and ski jumping) do reasonably well. Athletes whose sports do not involve the performance of activities similar to this test of courage, however, do not usually exhibit very much fortitude in this experimental situation. Thus the findings suggest that courage is specific to the sport.

fear they evidenced as recorded by the observing camera. There was a relationship between the measures of fear recorded and the ability to name the correct number exposed during each dive. The more fearful subjects were usually unable to report the number they were presented during their dives.

There were methodological problems inherent in this investigation, for no inter-trial reliabilities were obtained. At the same time there are many provocative ideas which might be explored in future research of this nature.

In general the experimenter concluded that coaches and physical educators cannot claim to be able to develop something generally termed "courage." Rather, they should specify courage in a particular situation.

Figure 7. Courage and the influence of stress upon perceptual judgments have been evaluated by requiring athletes to dive and to jump from 3-meter diving boards as shown. After leaving the board, the athlete is required to identify a number which is flashed at the same time his feet leave the platform. Other measures obtained in this experiment are the time between the "go" signal is given and the time the athlete leaves the board, and photographic evidence of anxiety reflected in facial and bodily postures assumed as the athlete is on the board.

Furthermore the experimental findings suggest that transfer of courage from one apparently dangerous activity to a second dangerous activity is not likely to occur unless the activities are highly similar.

The experimenter suggested that many people may feel fear and yet may somehow be able to overcome it in various situations. It is also apparent that courage is dependent upon many factors, including age, sex, social conditions, the presence of the opposite sex, and similar variables.

Further studies should attempt to determine how courage may be trained for in general and in specific sports situations. Other investigations might be concerned with differentiating between various kinds of courage and fears, including moral versus physical courage, specific versus general courage, and more subtle components of this elusive attribute.

It is likely that the fear of physical obstacles may be overcome by exposure to these same obstacles, wherein this exposure is in gradual stages. For example, in an observation with school children in Czechoslovakia, it was found that when confronted with a high-jump problem whose crossbar had the configuration ∧∧∧∧∧ , about 50 per cent refused to jump, even though all of them were willing to jump a level crossbar of the same height as the highest point of the irregularities contained on the first crossbar. (33) However, after a period of training, these same children all consented to jump the jagged crossbar.

On the other hand, moral fears, such as fear of speaking out and fear of committing a sin, are probably not overcome through physical education activities. Probably many coaches and physical educators believe that they may modify this type of moral courage through physical activities, but this is perhaps not possible, due to the fact that this type of moral courage is a more basic part of the child's and the adolescent's personality structure.

To develop a program in schools or in athletic training camps intended to enhance courage, a variety of stressful activities should be included. Perhaps by exposing children and more mature individuals to a number of tests of valor, some kind of general courage in the face of physical obstacles might be developed.

Further training in the building of self-confidence and courage in the performance of a variety of physical tasks by children should also take place in front of audiences of various types, including members of the opposite sex, with first a maximum and later a minimum of support from the instructor.

Within recent years improved technological advancements in the use of monitoring devices have opened up a new area of investigation. Small power packs strapped to the bodies of athletes have enabled them to move independent of complex apparatus which may produce visual and graphic displays of their heart rates, respiration characteristics, and other electrophysiological measures. Thus the levels of activation for action can be monitored while athletes are engaging in unimpeded action!

In 1960, Seliger examined for short periods of time the heart rates, the nature of expired air, and other physiological indices of soccer players and of volleyball players while these players were engaged in their games. (27) Husman in 1968 reported heart rate changes of a coach of swimming and of a coach of basketball. During stressful periods of competition, as in critical races and as in the ends of close basketball games, it was found that the heart rates of the coaches while watching the competition approximated those of their competing athletes who were engaged in violent exercise. (10) And prior to the Mexican Olympics most of the teams' physiologists monitored the physiological characteristics of their runners, using telemetric equipment of the type described.

The findings of a group of experiments in which superior athletes' frustrations and aspiration levels were evaluated also contain implications for the psychological preparation of athletes and for further research. In one study in this series, for example, eighty track-and-field athletes participated. (7) Using a back-leg-lift dynamometer, the subjects worked in pairs. One member of the pair was the "frustrated" subject one day, while the other subject was not; their roles were interchanged by the experimenter on the second day. Prior to being asked to exert maximum tension on the dynamometer, the athletes were asked to estimate how many pounds they expected to pull. It was possible for the experimenter to distort the pounds registering on an indicator which the subject could view so that the efforts exerted by either subject could be experimentally controlled either in an upward or in a downward direction. Thus on one day the "frustrated" subject viewed a score following his first trial which was less than the pressure he had actually exerted. The "nonfrustrated" subject was given his exact score following the first trial.

Following this type of experimental frustration, the subjects' behaviors were observed and rated. It was noted, for example, whether they withdrew from the task, whether they voiced their displeasure with their scores, and whether they requested additional trials. And the nature of their future estimates of performance was noted if the subjects decided to continue. The most important kind of data obtained in this experiment thus concerned the quality and the quantity of the subjects' reactions to frustration.

In general it was found that the aspiration levels of superior track-and-field athletes were influenced by failure and success experiences in the same manner as the aspiration levels of normal subjects were influenced. (8) It was typically found, however, that the reactions of superior athletes to frustration and to inferior performance were more volatile than those of a normal population. Specifically, sportsmen with neurotic tendencies, as assessed on a paper-and-pencil test, were more unstable, possessed a lower tolerance to frustration within the experimental context, and tended to lower their estimates more quickly after frustration in the strength task. And athletes who had been previously assessed as extroverts also expressed themselves more dynamically after frustration.

In general, all the athletes tended to raise aspirations after success and to lower aspirations after failure more erratically than would be expected in a normal population of young men, that is, a population of nonathletes. However, generalizing from the findings available is somewhat tenuous, since a population of nonathletes was not utilized in the study. Similarly it was difficult to separate the effects of competition from frustration under the experimental conditions described. Studies of the nature described, if repeated under more controlled circumstances, could yield valuable information about groups of athletes and about individuals on various types of teams.

Summary

The previous material makes it obvious that evaluation of and the prediction of competitive performances of athletes have the greatest validity if data from both laboratory and field experiments are combined. Furthermore, it is apparent that the usefulness of the laboratory data is dependent upon the ingenuity of the experimenter in replicating as exactly as possible the stimulus and response conditions confronting the athlete in competition.

If an undue amount of attention is given to the personality of the athlete without reference to reactions to stresses encountered in the competitions to which the athlete is exposed, then the information that is gained will be of meager value. However, more fruitful information is usually obtained if the nature of the sport and the reactions of the athlete within this context are evaluated.

Generally the available evidence indicates that batteries of tests may be constructed. These tests may range from specific and simple laboratory tests, in which a narrow range of attributes are evaluated, to the more complex laboratory and field experiences, in which both responses and thoughts about responses are assessed. And to provide helpful data, these batteries of tests should be carefully designed to evaluate the attributes needed in specific sports situations.

The complexity of the human action system, interacting with the athlete's cognitive and associational processes, makes it apparent that little predictive value may be obtained if such qualities as courage, aspiration level, and the like, are evaluated only within the confines of a single experimental situation.

Thus psychomotor and psychological preparation of athletes should be directed toward the specific needs of a given event. The assisting psychologist will gain the confidence of both the athlete and the coach to the extent that the training suggestions are concrete and are directed toward the obvious and observable components of the sport in which help is desired.

The next chapter contains specific ways in which the athlete may be psychologically prepared for competition, based upon some of the information outlined within this chapter.

REFERENCES

1. Bartusek, B. "Prispevek k Problematice Vyuziti Slova ve Sportovnim Treninku" (A Contribution to the Problems of Using Words in Sports Training), *Vedecke Zaklady Sportovniho Treninku* (The Scientific Bases of Sports Training), Prague, 1956.
2. Dobry, L.; Choutka, M.; and Kostka, V. *Sportovni Hry* (Sports Games). Prague: State Pedagogical Publisher, 1966.
3. Gagajeva, G. M. "Narusenie Dvizenij Pri Razdrazenii Vestibuljarnovo Apparata" (The Disorders of Movements During the Stimulation of the Vestibular Apparatus). *Ucenyje Zapisky/Gcolifk* (Scientific Contributions of the State Central Institute of Physical Culture), Moscow, 1, 1949.
4. Gagajeva, G. M. "Psichologiceskaja Charakteristika Futbola" (Psychological Characteristics of Soccer). *Psichogia Sporta* (Psychology of Sport), Moscow, 1959.
5. Geron, E.; Popov, N.; and Dimitrova, S. *Methods for Psychological Investigations*. Sofia: Medicina i Fizkultura, 1963.
6. Gikalov, V. "Jednoducha a Slozita Reakce v Cinnosti Lyzare" (The Simple and Complicated Reaction Time in Downhill Skiing). *Disertacni Prace*, Nepublikovano (Dissertation, Unpublished), Prague, 1968.
7. Hosek, V. "Posuny Aspiracni Urovne po Uspechu a Neuspechu Jako Vyraz Adaptace k Vykonu" (A Shifting of the Aspiration Level After Success and

Failure as an Indication of the Adaptation of Organism). *Teorie a Praxe Telesne Vychovy*, Prague, 14:5, 1966.

8. Hosek, V. "Vliv Uspechu a Neuspechu na Naslednou Dusevni Cinnost Sportovce" (The Influence of Success and Failure upon Succeeding Mental Activity of Athletes). *Sbornik Vedecke Rady UvCstv* (The Volume of the Czechoslovakian Scientific Council of the Czechoslovakian Committee of Physical Education), II, 27–44, 1966.

9. Hrase, J. "Vyuziti Aktivni Slovni Metody pri Nacviku Trojskoku" (The Use of the Active Word Method in Training the Triple Jump). *Studie z Pedagogiky a Psychologie* (Studies in Pedagogy and Psychology), Prague, 169–84, 1958.

10. Husman, B.; Hanson, D.; and Walker, R. "The Effect of Coaching Basketball and Swimming upon Emotion as Measured by Telemetry." Speech presented at the Second International Congress of Sports Psychology, Washington, D.C., November 1968.

11. Jegupov, L. F. "Takticeskije Ustanovki Slalomistov" (The Tactical Attitudes of the Slalom Skiers). *Voprosy Psichologii Sporta* (Questions of Sports Psychology), A. C. Puni (ed.), Moscow, 1955.

12. Jegupov, L. F. "Zapominanije Slalomnoj Trassy" (Recording of a Slalom Track). *Voprosy Psichologii Sporta* (Questions of Sports Psychology), A. C. Puni (ed.), Moscow, 1955.

13. Kocian, M. "Vliv Cilevedome Volni Aktivity na Zkvalitneni Vycviku v Behu na Stredni Vzdalenosti" (The Influence of Volitional Activity on the Higher Quality of the Training of Middle Distance Runners). *Teorie a Praxe Telesne Vychovy*, Prague, 4:229–37, 1962.

14. Krestovnikov, N. A. *Narys Fyziologie Telesnych Čuiceni* (The Outline of the Physiology of Physical Exercises). Prague, 1954.

15. Macak, I. "Vychova Pozornosti ve Volejbale" (The Education of Attention in Volleyball Games). *Teorie a Praxe Telesne Vychovy*, Prague, 3:8, 1955.

16. Macak, I. "O Koncetracii Pozornosti Hraca na Vykon vo Futbalovom Stretnuti" (About the Concentration of Attention of the Player on the Performance in a Soccer Game). *Trener a Čuicitel* (Trainer and Physical Education Instructor), Bratislava, 7:11, 1963.

17. Macak, I. "Problematiques des Recherches dans la Psychologie de l'Education Physique" (The Problems of Research in the Psychology of Physical Education). *Proceedings*, First International Congress of Sports Psychology, F. Antonelli (ed.), Rome, 1965.

18. Puni, A. C. "Ueber die Aktive Rolle der Vorstellungen bei der Aneignung von Bewegungsfertigkeiten" (Concerning the Active Role of Ideas in Motor Learning). *Teorija i Praktika Fiskultury*, Moscow, 9, 1947.

19. Puni, A. C. *Ocerki po Psichologii Sporta* (Sketches in Sports Psychology). Moscow, 1959.

20. Puni, A. C. "Bewegungsvorstellungen und Training" (Ideomotor Ideas and Training). *Beitrag zur Theorie de Koerperkultur* (Contribution to the Theory of Physical Culture), Berlin, 1961.

21. Rafalovitsch, A. G. "Znacenije Samostojatelnovo Opredelenija i Spravnitelnoj Ocenki Vremeni v Razvitii 'Cuštva Vremeni' u Begunov" (The Mean-

ing of Self-estimation of Time on the Development of the "Time Sense" in Runners). *Voprosy Psichologii Sporta* (Questions of Sports Psychology), Moscow, 1955.

22. Roudik, P. A. "Versuch Einer Methodik zur Untersuchung des Gleichgewichtsgefuhles" (The Methodical Attempt of Investigation of the Sense of Balance). *Psychomotorik und Koerperkultur* (Psychomotor and Body Culture), Moscow, 1935.

23. Roudik, P. A. *Psychologie* (Psychology), Prague, 1958.

24. Roudik, P. A. "Psichologija Sporta" (Sports Psychology). *Psichologiceskaja Nauka v S.S.S.R.* (Psychological Science in the U.S.S.R.), Moscow, II, 1960.

25. Roudik, P. A.; Puni, A. C.; et al. *Problemy Psichologii Sporta* (Problems of Sports Psychology). Moscow, Vols. 1 and 2, 1962.

26. Safarik, V. "Vysetreni Reakcni Doby Kosikaru" (The Investigations of Reaction Time of Basketball Players). Paper read at the Scientific Conference of Faculty of Physical Education and Sports, Prague, 1967.

27. Seliger, V. *The Physiology of Physical Exercises.* Prague, 1962.

28. Stransky, A. "Uloha Slovni Instrukce pri Vytvareni Pohyboveho Navyku" (The Role of Verbal Instruction upon the Automation of Movements). *Dissertation*, 1959: *Summary in Teorie a Praxe Telesne Vychovy*, Prague, 9, 1960.

29. Stransky, A. "Typy Slovnich Instrukci a Vyznam Jejich Sledovani pro Nacvik a Regulaci Specialnich Pohybovych Dovednosti" (The Importance of Research in Different Types of Verbal Instructions for the Training of Special Motor Skills). *Csl. Psychologie* (Czechoslovakian Psychology), 10:4, 1966.

30. Surkov, E. N. "O Roli Slova i Pokaza v Zapominanii Gimnasticeskich Upraznenij" (The Role of Words and of Demonstration in Recording of Physical Exercises). *Theorie und Praxis der Koerperkultur*, Berlin, 7, 1952.

31. Tschernikova, O. A. *Psichologiceskij Analiz Sportivnovo Bega* (The Psychological Analyses of Sport Runs). Moscow, 1957.

32. Vanek, M. "Vyzkum Odvahy a Strachu v Telesne Vychove" (Research on Courage and Fear in Physical Education). *Dissertation*, Prague, 1951; *Summary:* "Ein Beitrag zum Problem der Angst und des Mutes in der Koerperziehung" (A Contribution to the Problem of Fear and Courage in Physical Education). *Theorie und Praxis der Koerperkultur*, Berlin, 3:9, 1954.

33. Vanek, M. *Psychologicke Zaklady Telesne Vychovy* (The Psychological Basis of Physical Education). Prague: State Pedagogical Publisher, 1963.

34. Vanek, M., and Hosek, V. "Tachistoskopicke Vysetreni Hracu Jako Ukazatel Kvality Rozhodovani" (Tachistoscopic Investigations of Players as Indicators of the Quality of Their Judgment). Paper read at the meeting of Sports Psychologists in Harachov, Czechoslovakia, 1967.

CHAPTER 5

Personality Attributes of Athletes

and Sports Groups

Several theoretical approaches are to be found that relate the concept of personality to superior athletic performance. Neumann, for example, suggests that participation in high-level athletic competition provides an important positive addition to an individual's personality trait structure. He states that harmonious development of the personality comes about through sports participation. (11)

Steinbach, a psychiatrist, evidences another approach to personality-sports participation relationships. He writes, for example, that athletic participation is a form of compensation evidenced by individuals who lack a well-integrated personality. (18)

Stransky and Svoboda take a more complex look at the problem. They state that sports participation is one of several kinds of specific activities which men may be selected for and which they in turn select to participate in. In this theoretical framework, it is suggested that only certain personality types can undergo the social and physical stress of participation in highly competitive sports situations, and as continued participation is engaged in, the athlete in turn undergoes both negative and positive personality changes. (19)

Some controversy surrounds the question as to whether or not there is some kind of general personality trait pattern typical of athletes. Studies in the United States and in Europe often present findings which purport to identify an athletic type, or the emergence of specific personality trait factors within specific sports. When interpreting such findings, however, one must carefully consider the manner in which the researcher has defined the term "athlete," since there is no general agreement concerning just what an "athlete" is. In addition, the sample size is many times not representative and/or large enough. At the same time the nature of the culture within which the study has been carried out is important to consider. The cultural status given the sport, as well as the attendant political climate, prevalent weather, and similar conditions, can exert a marked influence upon the nature of the individuals taking part in sports, as well as the number of people who may be drawn to specific sports.

Furthermore, there is a lack of standardization of the various personality measures employed in various countries. At the same time, various modifications of similar-appearing tests will often produce confusing findings when the results of the two studies are compared. The nature of some of the measures used has been previously described, but the list is by no means an exhaustive one.

With these basic considerations in mind, the following information was derived from a review of the research concerning the personality of athletes, the nature of the personality traits generally found in various sports, and comparisons of athletes' personalities with norms. Comprehensive reviews of the literature on this topic covering research prior to 1960 have been written by Scott (16) and by Johnson and Cofer (2). A recent résumé of the available studies was compiled by Kane and Warburton (8).

In general, the findings of recent studies carried out in Europe and in the United States with large numbers of athletes indicate that the identification of a typical personality trait pattern expected to appear in an "athlete" is a tenuous undertaking. The trait patterns isolated in these investigations indicate that within certain sports groups, and on the part of certain individuals, expected personality traits may often be identified. But the delineating of some ubiquitous "animal" called an *athlete* cannot be done with any degree of certainty. If one compares personality measures of a large group of athletes from many different sports, it is likely that the average scores will approximate those found within a normal population of young men and women of a similar age and living in a similar culture.

In 1957 the German researcher Neumann (11) used three groups of subjects in a study of personality differences among "recreational" athletes and highly competitive athletes and nonathletes. Six observers were utilized and rated the subjects according to the extent to which they exhibited twenty-three personality traits. The observers watched the subjects in a similar sports situation contrived by the experimenter. Other measures obtained from the subjects were their responses to a Rorschach projective test and by a test of numerical ability.

Neumann's findings included the suggestion that the over-all personality score exhibited by the athlete groups were not significantly different from the total score obtained when observing the nonathletes. Specific differences were found, however, when certain personality traits were compared between the groups. Athletes were found to be more sociable, evidenced higher levels of what was termed "emotionality," were more practical in their approach to problems, and were more aggressive and more self-confident.

Similar to many European studies of this nature, no inter-observer reliabilities were reported, and at the same time no statistical verification was presented to confirm the significance of personality trait differences purportedly discovered between athletes and nonathletes.

In 1965, Seist (17) investigated the personality traits of seventy-seven of Austria's best athletes from a variety of sports. He employed a personality and interest test developed by the German psychiatrists Mittenecker and Toman, as well as a short form of the MMPI.

Seist found that the athletes he tested were characterized by high levels of self-criticism, and were more extroverted than the norms on these tests. Comparisons of sex differences within the groups revealed that the males were less neurotic than would be expected within a normal population. The male athletes seemed to be physiologically more stable under stress than the women athletes. Female athletes tended to be more susceptible to depression than were the male athletes, according to Seist's findings.

Again these findings should be evaluated carefully. Only one personality test was administered and, similar to the study reported by Neumann, only cursory statistical treatment was accorded the data (i.e., comparison of mean scores).

In London, England, Kane investigated three groups of track-and-field athletes in 1964 by means of the Cattell test previously described. (6) He found that, in general, distance runners were more introverted, but other competitive types were not identifiable with reference to the personality test scores. In a factor analysis of the Sixteen Item Cattell in 1966, Kane found that a "footballer type" was identifiable, and the factors which emerged included one that reflected a high degree of self-control. A second factor was an extrovertive trait reflecting urgency. A third factor was named "rough-mindedness." Kroll and Peterson in 1964, after comparing trait differences between winning and losing football teams, found that the former were generally composed of individuals who were more venturesome, had a higher degree of self-confidence and self-control. (13)

In Czechoslovakia, Brichcin and Kocian studied a group of long-distance runners with respect to personality and concluded that athletes selecting (or being selected for) this activity displayed marked introversion. (1) These latter researchers employed the Cattell test. Hosek, also from Czechoslovakia, examined eighty track-and-field athletes by the Mittenecker-Toman test as well as by Knobloch's questionnaire, evaluating neurotic tendencies, purportedly measuring whether or not the respondent was generally content or discontent with his life. Hosek found that the track-and-field athletes were more variable on the extroversion-introversion scale than are normals, with more scores locating themselves on the extremes of this scale. The athletes displayed more neurotic symptoms than would be found in a comparable group of nonathletes, and were not as sociable as would be expected of other young men their age who were not participating in athletics. (3) Hosek also found that the athletes were more self-critical and more extroverted as compared with normals. They were also found to be more stable physiologically, more sociable, but also evidenced a tendency to be discontent with their lot in life. They were also found to evidence fewer neurotic tendencies than would be found among a normal population. The track-and-field participants similarly displayed aggressive tendencies by their responses on the tools utilized.

Generally these and similar findings suggest that the superior athlete is not usually content, but instead may display aggressions and neurotic tendencies which he may be attempting to reconcile through sports. Athletes training for high-level competitive sport may often be preoccupied with their workouts, which prevents them from becoming well-rounded individuals with respect to academic attainment and to sociability.

From 1964 to 1968 an extensive study by Vanek and Hosek was carried out employing 260 athletes in ten sports, including track and field, cycling, ice hockey, wrestling, volleyball, weightlifting, archery, canoe-ing, and water skiing. This study is still in progress, and at the present time data from an additional 750 athletes are being analyzed. In the first part of the investigation both men and women athletes were ana-lyzed, including twenty-five women classified as the best female athletes in the country. The average age of the subjects evaluated was 23.5 years (S.D. 4.6 years). The findings reflect information concerning athletes as well as the validity of the tests used. For example, the scores ob-tained from the Eysenck and the Cattell tests in evaluating the same qualities (i.e., introversion and neuroticism) were similar (correlations ranged from 0.7 to 0.8). At the same time all the scores on the Eysenck and the Cattell tests obtained from athletes corresponded to the norms for each test, indicating few differences in personality trait structures when the total group of athletes was contrasted to the norms.

Specifically it was found that in some sports there was a trend toward extroversion, while in other sports there was a tendency toward higher stability. On the Cattell test only three differences were found when the athletes were compared to the norms. The athletes were a little more reserved, were more intelligent, and were more imaginative. The ice hockey players within this population were found to be higher in extroversion, lower in self-criticism, and evidenced lower neurotic tendencies.

Drs. Ogilvie and Tutko have reported a number of studies investigat-ing personality trait qualities of athletes in the United States. (12), (13) These have generally appeared in various speeches they have delivered and are not available to monitored research journals at this time. They have employed the Jackson Personality Research Form B, a special form of the Semantic Differential, and the Minnesota Multiphasic Per-sonality Inventory. The Cattell CPQ and the Cattell HSPQ have also been utilized to test young male swimmers.

In one investigation, Air Force cadets were compared with athletes at the Air Force Academy, and the latter were found to be more rule-bound, tough-minded, analytic, self-sufficient, and self-controlled. When these same cadets' scores were contrasted with scores obtained from a first-year football (American) team in a university of high academic standards, Ogilvie and Tutko found that the cadets were more stable emotionally, more self-assured, socially precise, and were significantly less anxious and tense.

In 1964 the United States male Olympic swimmers were also evaluated by Ogilvie and Tutko. (13) The group was further subdivided into those who had won gold medals ($N = 7$) and those who had not. The trends revealed were not statistically significant, due to the few number of subjects. However, they included the indication that the exceptionally talented swimmers were self-reliant, emotionally very stable, were liberal thinkers, and exhibited a great deal of self-control and self-discipline. The medalists tended to be lower in anxiety, lower in neuroticism, and were more independent, with an ability to handle emotional stress.

In another investigation by this same team of researchers from San Jose, California, a group of sixty-seven novice race car drivers were compared to a group of thirty-eight national competitors in this hazardous sport. The superior drivers were found to be more emotionally stable, more venturesome and bold, and more tough-minded and self-assured. Furthermore, the licensed drivers had a higher need for achievement, exhibitionism, autonomy, and dominance than did the less experienced race car drivers.

The Cattell CPQ was administered by Ogilvie and Tutko in 1967 to thirty-three boys (mean age 10.1) and to thirty-seven girls (mean age 9.8), who were members of a swim club preparing top-level performers in the United States (the Santa Clara Swim Club). Another fifty-one boys and girls on this same team (mean age 14) were administered the Cattell HSPQ. (12) Comparison of this data was also made with data collected on Olympic swimmers with an average age of 19.4. In general, the trends evidenced, from the ages of ten through nineteen years, were the following. The younger children were more introverted, while the scores collected from the older ones indicated that they were more outgoing and extroverted. Self-assertiveness also increased as a function of age; the younger swimmers were serious and sober-minded, while the older ones were happy-go-lucky in nature. The younger swimmers were found to be self-centered, while the older ones were not. The younger swimmers were lower in self-control and self-discipline than were the more experienced ones. The younger children evidenced more resting anxiety, while this was not marked in the more experienced competitors.

The researchers point out that interpretation of these findings must be carried out carefully. The study is not a longitudinal one, but a cross-sectional sampling; thus variables other than continued participation in competitive swimming could have caused the changes recorded, i.e., change in age, the elimination of the less capable performers, and so on.

The research program at San Jose has resulted in the collection of a large amount of data. What seems to be needed now is a standardization of testing instruments, the development of some kind of cogent theory, and publication of the findings in journals and in book form.

Recently an investigation by the Americans Kroll and Crenshaw, using 387 athletes, has offered further information concerning the personality trait structures of athletes within various competitive groups. (9) Using the multiple discriminant function analysis technique, significant profile differences were found for each of the four athletic groups studied. For example, football players and wrestlers were found to have similar personality profiles, while gymnasts and karate participants also were found to be similar in personality.

Relatively few studies have been carried out on the personality of women athletes. Exceptions are the investigations by Ogilvie and Tutko (13), by Kane (7), by Malumphy (10), and other unpublished studies covered in review by Cofer and Johnson (2) and others (8). The study by Ogilvie and Tutko was not aided by any statistical treatment of the data, but was a comparison of mean scores posted by male and by female age-group swimmers on a battery of personality tests. In addition, twenty San Jose State women competitors were administered three standard psychological paper-and-pencil tests (the Cattell 16 PF Forms A and B, the Jackson Personality Research Form B, and the Semantic Differential that the researchers designed for swimmers).

In general, they found that the scores of the female athletes differed from the male scores on traits which the society would define as feminine—i.e., the women were lower in dominance and aggression, while being more impulsive, sensitive, and high in succorance. Comparison of top-level swimmers by sex and age-group swimmers by sex indicated that the women tended to be more reserved, more deliberate, and at times more tense and driven. The findings outlined by Ogilvie and Tutko, when comparing men to women athletes, indicate that on feminine traits the women scored as expected.

Kane and Callaghan compared world-class women tennis players to players of less ability and found the former to be emotionally stable, to have self-confidence, and to be lower in frustration. (7)

A recent doctoral dissertation in the United States by Malumphy investigated the personality structure and background of 170 women participating in regional and national intercollegiate athletic events. (10) The Cattell 16 PH test and a personal information questionnaire designed by the investigator were utilized. It was found that women competing in different sports (golf, tennis, and "in an aquatic art symposium") were similar in the majority of personality traits, differing only as follows:

1. The aquatic competitors were less conscientious, self-sufficient, and less apprehensive than the golfers.

2. The tennis players were more conscientious and more emotionally stable than the controls.

3. The golfers were more venturesome, more apprehensive, and at the same time more controlled, as well as being more assertive than the other sportswomen and the controls.

Data from the personal questionnaire administered to her subjects revealed to Malumphy that two thirds believed that participation in their sport enhanced their feminine image; that one fifth felt that it made no difference, while only 6 per cent reported that they believed that participation in sport detracted from their images as women. Seventy-five per cent reported that "significant others" in their lives approved and encouraged their participation and competition.

Malumphy concluded that certain personality traits may be prerequisite for success in the various sports assessed by women competitors; and that avoidance of sports in the United States by women, in order not to detract from their feminine image, is not a sound course of action. (10)

Summary

A survey of the research revealed few continuous and extensive research programs evaluating personality characteristics of large groups of athletes, with the exception of the programs of Ogilvie and Tutko, and of Vanek and Hosek. Yet even these programs at times lack coherence. The data emanating from studies of the psychologists from San Jose are often treated in a cursory manner (i.e., multiple tests are used instead of variance techniques), while the data from the work of the Europeans are even less likely to have received any kind of viable statistical evaluation. It is believed that in future work the following objectives might be attained:

1. The selection of athletes, particularly in countries relatively short of

talent, may be made more objective by encompassing assessment procedures involving personality trait measures. (4)

2. The "problem athlete" may become more easily identifiable and thus as the result of further research, data may be forthcoming which will aid the athlete in rather direct ways.

3. A valid classification of sports events, based upon psychological traits needed to perform them, might be developed.

4. The efficiency of future athletes might be enhanced when various personality trait data are compared to psychomotor test data.

5. With the world standardization of personality measures, valid intercultural studies involving comparisons of sports populations exposed to various economic, cultural, political, and climatic conditions may be carried out.

6. The findings derived from studies of athletes' personalities may make a significant contribution to the entire theoretical sphere of the study of personality.

REFERENCES

1. Brichcin, M., and Kocian, M. "Vysledky Psychologickeho Vysetreni Bezcu Vytrvalcu" (The Results of Psychological Investigations of Long-Distance Runners). *Problemy Psychologie Osobnosti* (The Problems of the Personality Psychology), Prague: Academia, I, 161–66, 1967.
2. Cofer, C., and Johnson, W. R. "Personality Dynamics in Relation to Exercise and Sports," in *Science and Medicine of Exercise and Sport*, W. R. Johnson (ed.). New York: Harper Brothers, 1960.
3. Hosek, V. "Zjistovani Nekterych Vlastnosti Osobnosti u Sportovcu" (An Investigation of Some Personality Traits of Superior Athletes). *Teor. a Praxe Tel. Vych.*, Prague, **13**:1, 1965.
4. Hosek, V., and Man, F. "Pripominky k Vyberu Talentu z Psychologickeho Hlediska" (Some Remarks About Talent Selection from the Psychological Point of View). *Metodicky Dopis Sekce Kanoistiky* (Newsletter of the Czechoslovakian Canoeing Federation), Prague, 1968.
5. Kane, J. E. "Personality and Physical Ability." Paper read at the Second International Congress of Sports Psychology, Washington, D.C., 1968.
6. Kane, J. E. "Personality and Physical Ability." *Proceedings, Sport Sciences Conference*, Tokyo, 1964, 201–08.
7. Kane, J. E., and Callaghan, J. L. "Personality Traits in Tennis Players." *British Lawn Tennis*, July 1965.

8. Kane, J. E., and Warburton, F. W. "Personality Relates to Sport and Physical Ability," in *Readings in Physical Education.* London: Physical Education Association, 1966.

9. Kroll, Walter, and Crenshaw, William. "Multivariant Personality Profile Analysis of Four Athletic Groups." Paper read at the Second International Congress of Sports Psychology, Washington, D.C., 1968.

10. Malumphy, Theressa. "The Assessment of Personality and General Background of Women Participating in Regional and National Intercollegiate Competition." Unpublished paper, Graduate School, University of Oregon, 1968.

11. Neumann, O. *Sport und Personlichkeit. Versuch einer psychologischen Diagnostik mit Deutung der Personlichkeit des Sportlers* (Sport Activity and Personality. The Use of a Psychological Assessment to Evaluate the Personality of Athletes), Munich, 1957.

12. Ogilvie, B. C. "Psychological Consistencies Within the Personality of High-Level Competitors." *J. Am. Med. Assn.,* Special Olympic Year Edition, September–October 1968.

13. Ogilvie, B. C.; Tutko, T. A.; and Young, I. "Comparison of Medalists, Non-Medalists, Olympic Swimmers." *Am. J. Sports Medicine,* 1966.

14. Ohkawa, N. "A Study of General Traits and Syndromes of First-Class Sportsmen in Japan." *Proceedings* of the Sports and Sciences Conference, Tokyo, 1964, 189–98.

15. O.S.S. (Office of Strategic Services). *The Assessment of Men.* New York: Holt, Rinehart, 1948.

16. Scott, M. G. "The Contributions of Physical Activity to Psychological Development." *Res. Quart.,* 31:2, 307–20, 1960.

17. Seist, H. "Die psychische Eigenart der Spitzensportler" (Psychic Particularities of Superior Athletes). *Zeitschrift der diagnostischen Psychologie und Personlichkeitforschung* (Journal of Diagnostic Psychology and Personality), Vienna, 2, 1965.

18. Steinbach, M. "The Personality of the Superior Athlete." Lecture given in Zurich, June 1968.

19. Stransky, A., and Svoboda, B. "Osobnost ve Sportovni Cinnosti" (Personality in Sport Activity). *Csl. Psychologie* (Czechoslovakian Psychology, 11:1, 1967.

20. Vanek, M., and Hosek, V. "Methodological Problems of Psychodiagnostic Investigations of the Personality of the Superior Athlete." Paper read at the Second International Congress of Sports Psychology, Washington, D.C., 1968.

CHAPTER 6

Motives of Superior Athletes

Since the beginnings of experimental psychology, attempts have been made to measure motivation. The tools used have ranged from projective tests to questionnaires containing questions both subtle and obvious in nature. Within the past years, European sport psychologists have used various approaches in the evaluation of motivational structures of athletes, of motivational changes over times, of motivational differences in superior and apprentice performances, and intersport differences in motive systems. (2) These investigations have not been pursued for long, and this area of study is still in its infancy.

The nomenclature utilized in various countries in the study of motives makes comparisons of the findings difficult. The Russian literature is replete with investigations of "will power." (8) These studies have hinged upon various qualities underlying will power as well as upon methods of improving the will power of various athletes. These studies were carried out in Russia for a five-year period, during the early 1960's, in an intensive manner. Other countries in Europe have at times adopted this concept, and have at times integrated concepts of moral-political-ideological preparation with concepts of will power and motivation.

At times, studies of motives have been prompted by evaluating the findings of various personality studies that have already been reviewed. A great deal of information dealing with motive structures has been gained from autobiographies, from self-reports concerning values, motives, and fluctuations in attitudes, and from prolonged in-depth interviews between athlete and psychologist. (3), (4) These approaches have been employed by behavioral scientists in Europe who generally rejected the more global terms of will power, moral training, and the like as being too imprecise.

Multifactor theories of motivation have been constructed by some, attempting to explain many variables that impinge upon an athlete's inclination to perform. (10) Among the factors considered within such theories are body structure and physiological make-up, temperament, character, intelligence, basic physical abilities, skill, past experiences, aspiration level, and the like. A diagram of such an approach is shown in Figure 8.

The Figure suggests that a number of factors, located at the top of the diagram, contribute to performance. Furthermore, the final shaping of performance is primarily dependent upon aspiration level, which in turn molds the intensity of the effort expended. Moreover, the diagram presents the concept of feedback in so far as an individual, after judging the relative success or failure of his efforts, probably undergoes some kind of shift in some of the motives that determine his actions after most performance trials.

Investigations by Vanek and Hosek, in which the motives of over 600 athletes were studied, resulted in the schema shown in Figure 9, which attempts to depict primary, secondary, and social motives that impinge upon sports performance. (12)

In the center of the cluster are the general motives involving the need for physical activity and the need for achievement. It is hypothesized that these two undifferentiated motives are present in all individuals to varying degrees.

The degree to which an individual seeks and needs motor activity, of course, depends upon age, environment, and his general style of life. It is likely that environmental factors determine just what sport an athlete chooses, yet at the same time the strength of the motive determines the choice of some type of vigorous activity. Early success and failure experiences, of course, determine whether or not a given activity is pursued during childhood and adolescence.

Coaches working with young children should therefore attempt to present situations to children in which success when realized would provide the encouragement needed to give the child the desire to strive in a given activity. Thus the need is evidenced in general ways when the

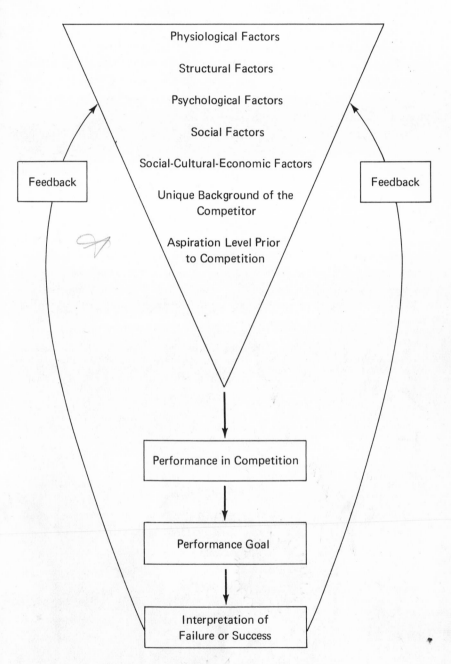

Figure 8. A multifactor theory of motivation.

child is younger, and it becomes increasingly specialized and directed as he matures.

Closely related to the need for activity is the need for achievement. This need has only been measured in imprecise ways, because European psychologists have not applied the more sophisticated measures of aspiration utilized within recent years by American psychologists and psychometrists.

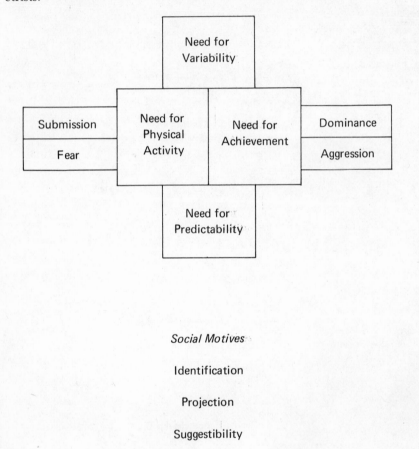

Social Motives

Identification

Projection

Suggestibility

Imitation

Competitiveness

Empathy

Figure 9. A cluster of primary motives of athletes.

These two basic needs interact with other basic tendencies, probably inborn or developing very early in life, that are placed adjacent to each other in Figure 9. The tendency to be either submissive or dominant here is represented by a continuum. Submission is closely aligned with the tendency to imitate, while dominance is sometimes paired with aggression.

Fear may be manifested in a number of ways, such as in direct aggression, in passivity, and in some combination of these types of reactions. In addition, fear may be considered to be in several different classification systems. For example, it has been found in depth interviews that not only are many athletes afraid of losing but, on the other hand, some are afraid of winning! It has been hypothesized by some, following in-depth interviews with athletes, that many seem to prefer to lose when victory seems at hand. It has been assumed that this fear may be caused by the fact that winning brings with it a number of responsibilities of which the athletes are well aware, especially the responsibility to continue winning. At the same time it is well known to the athletes that to be a winner is not always popular, and that often those cheering the winner are the first to deride subsequent losing efforts.

Fear can also be classified according to intensity—from mild apprehensive reactions to an objective healthy fear of an impending event. It may result either in an unusual amount of vigorous and unreasonable movement or in a kind of immobile incapacity to move almost as if the individual were unconscious. The former vigorous phenomenon has been termed *Bewegungssturm,* or "storm of movement," by Kretschmer. (5) The latter immobile phenomenon has been termed *Platzangst,* or "top anxiety," by Kretschmer. (5)

In addition to this kind of observable fear, an athlete may be plagued with various subtle and general anxieties. These could involve some kind of unreasonable fear of social conditions, political situations, family background, and the like. Athletes find these anxieties more difficult to overcome than the more obvious fears described in the previous paragraph, which are more readily observed and corrected. If these anxieties are intense enough, they may be manifested in various neurotic and psychotic states. This type of individual may become discoordinated and may evidence what has been termed an "effect syndrome," which is marked by breathlessness, fatigue, and the like, for which there is no apparent reason.

Anxiety, in a number of studies with athletes in Europe and in the United States, has also been divided into situational and general anxiety. (1) It is common to see athletes evidence feelings of anxiety as they enter the stadium and/or are exposed to crowds. Thus, as sports become more emphasized and as more pressure is placed upon winning in both professional and so-called amateur competitions, it is probable that sports, which formerly provided a release for anxiety, may now tend to heighten anxiety in individuals participating.

Another system within the cluster of motives impinging upon athletes involves their need for variability and novelty of experience versus their need for stability and predictability of the situations in which they find themselves. It is usual to find that individual sports competitors, such as runners, gymnasts, divers, and the like, have a greater need for, and tolerance of, stability and predictability. On the other-hand, team-sport members are usually found to seek novelty and complexity.

However, in most sports activities both novelty and stability are found. In a team sport the dimensions of the field, the goals, and the rules remain constant from competition to competition, no matter where it is held. But during the competitions the situations confronting athletes are constantly changing. Thus superior athletes in most sports should be adaptable to and tolerant of both the sameness as well as to the ever-changing complexities and novelties of the situations in which they find themselves and which they create.

Figure 9 also includes important social motives which involve interpersonal reactions. These interpersonal reactions include needs for identification, intuition into the emotional states of others, suggestibility, and the projection of feelings to others.

It is common, for example, to see coaches project their fears into their players in harmful ways. On the other hand, it may be helpful if the players on one team are given the realization that the players on the other team may be experiencing the same feelings of fear and tension. In essence they may gain the ability to project their own feelings of anxiety into their opponents and to reduce their own feelings of fear and anxiety about the impending competition.

Some atheletes may also have the ability to intuitively know how other athletes whom they are meeting in competition may feel. With this kind of insight a superior athlete may, for example, further discourage his less capable opponents by a show of unusual lack of concern prior to or during a race. Knowing that they are fearful of him, he may take advantage of his insight and instill harmful fears into his adversaries.

Athletes to various degrees are suggestible. Some are easily influenced by teammates, coaches, and others with whom they come into social contact. On the other hand, some are not as easily influenced and tend to "keep their own councils" concerning training techniques, strategies, and other variables influencing performance.

Identification, within Vanek's system of motivation, suggests that some athletes align themselves at the emotional level very closely with their country, team, and/or coach. At times this identification may exist between a novice and a more superior athlete. A helpful motivational state may thus be constituted as the beginning performer attempts to emulate his more proficient "idol."

These latter four motives are likely to be more influenced by the social climate, whereas the central motives found in Figure 9 and discussed initially are more likely to be based upon biological and physiological factors. The strengths of the social motives, in turn, may influence the more basic motives, as a kind of feedback is effected between the more peripheral social motives and the more central biological-psychological ones. Thus the dynamics of the entire motivational structure are likely to be influenced by the changes in the projective, intuitive, and suggestive states of the performer.

A sensitive athlete assuming a leadership role, who is able to project his feelings into others on a team and who is dominant and without fear himself, may aid the others to deal with fear and anxiety contingent with the cluster of primary motives. (12) In addition, one may identify many kinds of secondary motives, including motives aligned with the social and economic advantages he might derive from his athletic successes. Sport activity may lead toward opportunities to travel, and thus provide a kind of secondary motive. An athlete may form useful social and economic "contacts" through his efforts in competitive sport.

Evaluation of the motives of an athlete or of a group of athletes in a given situation is extremely difficult, as many variables impose upon the measures obtained. Each individual is surrounded by a constellation of values, any one of which may impinge upon him at a given moment in time. The social and economic backgrounds of the athletes as contrasted to the social, political, and economic conditions prevalent in their countries will also influence to a marked degree that which they consider important.

Vanek further has developed a schema describing the types of motives generally impinging upon athletes during various stages in their lives and careers. (12) His theoretical formulations were influenced by ideas previously advanced by the Russian Puni, but he has attempted to elaborate on Puni's concepts.

The first category has been identified as the "Generalization" stage. During the early years of life the athlete is probably influenced by generalized configurations of motives, including inclinations for a number of

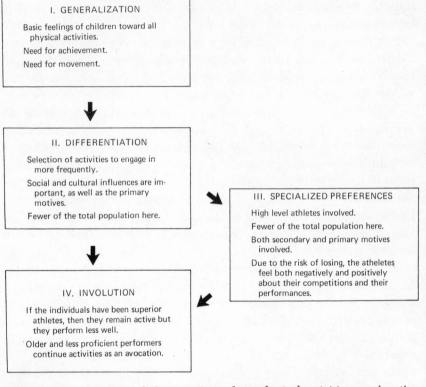

Figure 10. *Motivational changes of people in physical activities as a function of age.*

activities involving movement. He may at this point either seek out or tend to reject vigorous motor activity as a means of expressing himself. He may decide upon several types of activities within general classifications, such as team games, individual activities, and track-and-field events.

The second category has been identified as the "Differentiation" stage. The athlete's general need for achievement and for movement now begins to fragment and he becomes more selective of the sports in which he engages, of the level of competition in which he takes part, and of the types of training he decides to undergo. As the selection process continues, he will reject activities in which he experiences unpleasant outcomes and will retain his interests in those which give him pleasure. A number of secondary social motives impinge upon his performances and selections of activities at this stage.

The third category has been identified as the "Specialized Preferences" stage. The activity selected becomes more specific. While the primary motives still persist, there is an increasing influence of secondary motives. During this period, attitudes of the athlete may turn from positive to negative. His anxiety and apprehension may increase, as in reaching the top levels of competition. A selection process is going on during this period, and tends to reduce the number of competitors. He may become bored or "stale" when competing, and may need frequent short or prolonged rests.

The fourth category has been identified as the "Involution" stage. Performance is still at a high level, but there is a greater tendency to evidence regression. The athlete is motivated at this level by secondary motives, but at times he regresses to dependency upon more basic motives encountered at the initial levels, including aspiration and the need for mastery. However, he is more likely to identify intellectually the influence of his social and biopsychological motives during this stage than he was likely to do when he was younger. Thus these motives reappear, but at another level of consciousness. The athlete also is beginning to age, and thus he may continue to be motivated because he may desire to maintain the vigor and general fitness which he maintained during the previous stages described. Thus motivation during this period may depend more upon events intrinsic to the task than upon materials and social rewards extended from an external source. But the pleasure of competition may not be as strong during this phase as is the pleasure of movement for its own sake.

Thus Vanek maintains that the development of patterns of motivation in athletes may be graphed in the form of a spiral. The tail of the diagram meets the end as the athlete during the latter stages of competition becomes more likely to be influenced by the motives which initially impelled him to strive in athletic endeavors. Many people who do not achieve extremely high performance may also tend to "jump across" category three (Specialized Preferences) and enter the Involution stage. The motives important during the last stage of Involution are those which are more likely to be seen in individuals pursuing leisure-time activities, who may or may not have ever participated as top-level athletes.

Vanek maintains that when top athletes must inevitably pass from stage three to stage four, it is common to observe them undergoing a great deal of psychological stress. Their self-images may be threatened, and, if so, then they must change; and this change is not always easy for top athletes to undergo. At times the amount of conflict this involves may even be evidenced in successful or in unsuccessful attempts at self-destruction. Among top athletes, Vanek has found, there is a low incidence of psychoses; yet, at the same time, the incidence of suicides among top athletes in Europe, after competition, is significantly above what would be expected to occur by chance within a normal population of comparable ages. Unless an athlete has a sound philosophical perspective at this point in his life and foresees his changing role as a man, he is likely to encounter mild to severe adjustment problems. He should be permitted, and be given every assistance, to retreat from glory gracefully.

It is not frequently the practice to employ former athletes or coaches during this latter period of their lives. They may not, however, function well as coaches if their value system does not encompass the need to serve others. At the same time, superior athletes may lack the academic background which could qualify them for leadership roles in sport.

During the initial three stages within this schema, Vanek contends, the athlete must also be subjected to careful guidance. The amount of success and failure he is experiencing must be made clear to him; in this way he will be able to assess in exact manner whether or not he should continue to strive or should be content to settle for competition at less intense levels. The athlete should thus be prevented from overestimating as well as from underestimating his potential during the early periods of his life, as indulgence in these practices often leads to less emotional and intellectual maturity later. If an athlete's endeavors are not placed in good perspective by coaches, then it could lead to more attrition within the ranks of athletes than is caused by the natural selection process inherent in competition.

The athlete during this period must be prepared psychologically as well as socially to meet the changing demands made upon him and to channel his energies into what for him may constitute more productive athletic or intellectual endeavors. Vanek concludes that if the athlete advances too rapidly, the frustration he may incur may diminish his chances for real success and lessen his efforts in immediate sports competitions.

Professor Roudik, the Russian sport psychologist, has also derived a schema with which to explain the motivations of superior athletes. (9) According to Roudik, there are both indirect and direct motives to consider.

Roudik's list of indirect motives includes the achievement of health through sport, preparation for life's work, early success in school sports, and ideological and political motives associated with social objectives. The relative importance of these motives, Roudik asserts, as did Vanek, changes according to the success the performer achieves. Groups of motives impinge upon the athlete at various stages of his development, Roudik suggests.

Roudik's list of direct motives includes pleasure in movement, mastery over difficult and complex physical situations, aesthetic satisfaction in movement, the overcoming of fear of failure, pleasure from competition, and pleasure of winning and of demonstrating superior performance in national and world competitions.

The beginning athlete, says Roudik, has only a diffuse interest in sport activities in general, and does not concentrate upon a single one of them in which to achieve excellence.

The early stages of development, according to Roudik, are marked by the direct motives outlined above. Generally the environment will impose upon the younger athlete the sport in which he will participate, rather than the athlete being the sole influence in choosing a sport. A child raised in the mountains will ski, just as a child raised near water will swim. Thus during the formative years the sport imposes itself upon the child, and he is often obliged to perform in a given activity despite his personal preferences.

The second developmental level, according to Roudik, has been termed the stage of "specialization" in one sports activity. An important motive during this stage is the selection of a single sports activity in which to achieve excellence. The athlete attempts to reach higher and higher levels of proficiency, and more and more there is a matching of unique personality and emotional traits to the sports activity. Activity and success "feed back" into the athlete's motivational system; thus his aspiration level is generally raised, and he continues to seek increasingly higher levels of proficiency.

The final developmental level, according to Roudik, has been termed the stage of "superiority" in one sports activity. The athlete attempts to maintain and to extend his level of dominance in the sport. He attempts to achieve success not only for himself but for his homeland. He may attempt to find new techniques and tactics to enrich and to expand general and specific knowledge in his chosen sporting event. Roudik concludes that generally this knowledge will be transmitted to the younger athlete following in the footsteps of the superior athlete.

In general the schema outlined by Roudik parallels in several ways the conceptual framework offered by Vanek. Vanek's concept of diffusion of interest is similar to Roudik's ideas on this topic. At the same time Vanek's fourth stage has no counterpart in Roudik's framework of motives. Both theoretical frameworks, however, offer only a beginning from which future studies may emanate.

REFERENCES

1. Hosek, V. "Uzkost Vrcholovych Sportovcu a Moznosti Jejiho Zvladnuti" (Anxiety of Superior Athletes and Possibilities of Its Management). *Teorie a Praxe Telesne Vychovy*, Prague, **16**:7, 1968.
2. Linhart, J. *Psychologie Uceni* (The Psychology of Learning). Prague: State Pedagogical Publisher, 1967.
3. Kittler, J. "Zajem o Telesnou Vychovu u Zaku Vseobecne Vzdelavaci Skoly" (Interest in Physical Education by the Students in the General Public Schools). *Teorie a Praxe Telesne Vychovy*, Prague, 154–64, 1961.
4. Kocian, M. "Telovychovne Zajmy Mladeze ve Veku 16 az 18 Let" (Interest in Physical Education of Youth at the Age of 16 to 18). *Teorie a Praxe Telesne Vychovy*, Prague, **16**:7, 1968.
5. Kretschmer, E. *Koerperbau und Charakter* (Body Build and Character). Berlin, 1944.
6. Kunath, P. *Psychologie, Anleitung fur das Fernstudium* (Psychology, Introduction for Extramural Studies). Leipzig, 1963.
7. Puni, A. C. *Abriss der Sportpsychologie* (The Outline of Sports Psychology). Berlin: Volkseigener Verlag, 1962.
8. Puni, A. C. "O Strukture Volevych Kacestv Sportsmena i Planirovanii ich Rozvitija v Processe Trenirovki" (The Structure of the Attributes of the Athlete's Will Power and the Plan of His Development in Training). *Teorija i Praktika Fizkultury*, Moscow, **27**:3, 1964.
9. Roudik, P. A. *Psychologie: Ein Lehrbuch fur Turnlehrer, Sportlehrer und Trainer* (Psychology: A Textbook for Physical Educators, Sports Teachers and Coaches). Berlin: Volkseigener Verlag, 1963.
10. Severova, M. *Zavislost Vykonu Cloveka na Motivaci* (The Dependence of

Human Performance upon Motivation). Prague: Czechoslovakian Academy of Sciences, 1960.

11. Stransky, A. *Psychologie Sportu* (Psychology of Sports). Prague: State Physical Education Publisher, 1962.
12. Vanek, M. "Teorie Psychologicke Pripravy Sportovce" (Theory of Psychological Preparation of the Athlete). Dissertation for Associate Professor Degree, Philosophical Faculty, Prague, 1964.

PSYCHOLOGICAL
PREPARATION
OF THE SUPERIOR
ATHLETE

THE TERM "psychological preparation" appeared in the Russian literature in the early 1960's, and is contained in the works by Roudik and Puni. (Ch. 7, 11) During the intervening years others in Eastern Europe have used the term in their writings. And other scholars in Western Europe have used different words to denote a similar concept, such as "psychosomatic training," "psychotonic training," and "psychological training."

The Russians, in general, have employed the idea of psychological preparation in a specific manner, denoting the preparation for a single sports competition. The general psychological preparation of the athlete over a long period of time was referred to as "volitional-moral preparation."

Other writers in Eastern Europe, however, have attached a broader meaning to the term psychological preparation. Vanek, for example, has suggested that psychological preparation refers to both immediate and long-term general and specific psychic training of superior athletes. (Ch. 7, 14) And it is this latter meaning that the present writers have accorded to the term psychological preparation.

Psychologists in Europe evaluate athletes prior to competition with various performance tests. After evaluating them in this manner, decisions are made concerning how each individual should be prepared. In general it is found that athletes may be classified according to the amounts of performance tension they exhibit. Following competition this same information is utilized in order to dispel post-performance tensions of various kinds.

The material which follows has been divided into several sections. Initially the manner in which athletes are evaluated prior to competition is covered. Secondly the ways in which athletes are classified, based upon this data, are discussed. Finally the types of psychological preparation applied to each type of athlete are outlined.

CHAPTER 7

Pre-Competition Psychological Preparation

of the Superior Athlete

Pre-Performance Evaluation of Athletes

PSYCHOPHYSIOLOGICAL TESTS. The initial testing of individuals prior to competition took the form of physiological tests. These include the assessments of biochemical changes, of pulse rate fluctuations, of blood pressure modifications, and of respiratory fluctuations, which were all due to the stresses of impending competition. Some of the pioneers of these pre-competitive evaluations were the German Brustmann and the Russian Krestovnikov and his pupils in Moscow and in Leningrad. (1), (4)

Experiments of this type of pre-performance mobilization took several forms. Athletes were sometimes prepared for an activity of a given effort level and were carefully monitored physiologically while this information was given to them. After they seemed to prepare themselves for this initial level of performance, they were suddenly informed that they would have to work harder, such as to run faster or farther; and in some cases they were informed that less effort would have to be expended. During these changes in the amount of intensity for which the athletes were being "set," they were monitored, and various indices of the raising and lowering of physiological processes could be plotted as a function of the amounts of intensity for which the athletes were adjusting themselves. (5)

In similar experiments, athletes were informed that they were to compete in all-out efforts at a given time of the day; and when that time arrived, they were suddenly informed that competition would occur at a later time. Physiological processes were plotted and curves were obtained which reflected their cardiovascular accommodations to the expected times of competition and to the changed times of competition to which they were later exposed. (16)

Several findings arose from these experiments. In general the fluctuations seen in the physiological measures as a function of the amount, intensity, duration, or time effort were expected and were a highly individual matter. Some athletes tended to lower their levels of readiness when they were informed that competition would be postponed, while others maintained a high level of readiness. And some athletes successfully adjusted their levels of physiological preparedness upward when they were informed that more work would be required of them, while others either did not do so or could not do so.

It was found, as might be expected, that the better athletes had two major characteristics: (a) they could adjust their levels of preparedness to that commensurate with the intensities of the tasks they were facing, and they could easily adjust, either upward or downward, when the task demands were suddenly changed; (b) they could maintain their levels of preparedness high during the time interval separating the initial time of expected competition and the adjusted time of actual competition.

Psychomotor measures. About 1930, Puni in Leningrad, Roudik and his pupil Gernikova in Moscow, as well as psychologists in other European countries, began to evaluate the pre-performance states of athletes on various psychological measures. (9), (13) These measures were often correlated to physiological indices of activation.

The tests these psychologists used to evaluate the pre-performance readiness of athletes included what was termed a "coordination meter." In this task two rods were used, wherein one was held in each hand. These were guided simultaneously through two pathways on a desktop maze. Contact frequency and speed were evaluated. Concentration tests were also employed. A grid containing numbers in random order was placed in front of the athlete. The athlete was required to touch in numerical order each of the squares, and was timed to the nearest tenth of a second. Figure cancellation tests were also employed in a similar manner. In these, each "a" or "b" from a line of newsprint was to be canceled out, and a speed and accuracy score was obtained. These tests were administered at varying intervals prior to the start of competition. One might be administered several days before competition. Another administration might occur within hours, while the final trials might be given within minutes of the start of the athletic effort.[1]

In general it was found that disruption of coordination in the various tests was greatest in athletes who believed themselves to be unprepared for the impending athletic events. (15) The concentration tasks were similarly carried out well by the athletes who were well prepared and trained, and by students who felt that they were able to do well in the subject matter examinations. The subjects' preferences for physical performance over mental performance were also variables in producing differences in the various psychomotor tests and concentration tests that were administered. Individuals who preferred athletic competition were not disrupted, if prior to competition they were given various psychomotor tests, while those who did not prefer athletic competition were distracted by this type of pre-contest testing program.

The individuals who did better in competition on both mental and motor tasks were those who also did better in the various pre-performance tasks. Each task was viewed by the more successful athletes as simply one of a series of tasks to surmount. Studies of Czechoslovakian gymnasts confirmed the assumption that pre-performance disruption reflected in poor scores on coordination tasks and on tasks purportedly measuring concentration was predictive of poor athletic performances, while more successful performances in these tasks were predictive of good effort.

Summary

Several conclusions were derived from these interesting psychophysiological and psychomotor experiments which were administered to athletes just prior to competition. (6), (13), (14)

1. An optimum amount of pre-task tension was useful, and without this tension excellent performance could not be realized by the athletes tested.

[1] Vanek carried out experiments in which physiological as well as these psychomotor performance tests were given before athletic competition, before rigorous subject matter examinations, and before the threat of impending electrical shock. In general, the disruptive effects of performance tests, athletic competition, and electrical shock threat were similar.

Figure 11. Numerous psychomotor experiments have been carried out in the laboratory with athletes to determine their basic motor abilities, as well as to see how these attributes change prior to and after competition. The experiment shown requires a continuous complex response from the subject. At the same time the experimenter may apply an electric shock stresser to the subject's fore-arm. Thus both speed and accuracy (times the hand-held ring touches the complex track) may be scored as a function of learning, and as influenced by the stress imposed.

2. Using these tests, three pre-task states were able to be identified: (a) the athlete whose level of activation was close to optimum for the demands of the impending task; (b) the athlete whose level of activation was too low for the demands of the impending task; (c) the athlete whose level of activation was too high for the demands of the impending task.

3. Optimum arousal levels were highly individual matters. Some athletes needed to evidence fear and muscle tremor prior to competition, while others required a relatively calm state before performing. Thus each coach and each athlete were given guidelines concerning these individual differences in activation level which would produce the best effort for each athlete.

4. Observations of the curves of activation prior to competition in athletics led to the formulation of several phases in pre-performance ten-

sion. (a) Initially when the athlete first learns that he is to compete, or when he is selected for a national team, the activation curve begins to climb slowly upward. This has been referred to as the period of long-term tension. It is during this period of time that the athlete's motivation is high and that he trains hard to prepare himself for the impending events. (b) The initial period is followed by a period of time, a day or two prior to competition, which has been termed "pre-start tension." This is usually marked by a sudden swing upward of the curve of activation, and may be accompanied by little effort in actual physical training. (c) This period, just minutes prior to performance, is called "start tension," and usually occurs when the athlete comes into contact with the environment in which competition is to take place, as when he enters a stadium.

5. Competition tension occurs during the actual performance of the event, and may be in some activities, such as the 100-meter run, of shorter duration; and in other activities, such as soccer or football, of longer duration. This type of tension is influenced by the situation as it develops in the game; that is, whether or not the athlete is winning, losing, failing, or exceeding the goals he has set for himself.

6. Following competition, post-tensions are recorded that relate to what has just occurred in the performance situation, and that in turn influence the long-term tensions engendered by the athlete prior to future competitive efforts.

7. Post-task tension usually takes one of several forms. (a) Aggression will occur, particularly if the athlete has not done well or if the team has lost. Aggression, in turn, may take either of two forms: *extra-punitive*, in which aggression is directed against conditions and other people; and *intra-punitive*, in which aggression is directed against himself, as self-blame. (b) Depression and (c) euphoria are reactions that are highly individual and may take several forms within the same individual following the same contest or following different contests.

Reviewing these findings, the reader might ask himself at what point during these various phases of the activation curve the coach and the psychologist may be most helpful to the athlete prior to competition. Should their primary efforts be placed during the early part of the curve just after the athlete has realized that he will face the high-level competition? Should emphasis upon psychological preparation be placed during the pre-task tension period? What roles should the coach and the psychologist play during the post-task period of activation?

Of equal importance is the question of what, if anything, should be done during these various periods by the coach and the psychologist attempting to ready their athletes for optimum effort. The answers to some of the questions will be explored on the pages that follow.

Psychological Preparation During the Period of Long-Term Tension

This period begins when the athlete first realizes, sometimes many months or many years in advance, that he is to compete in high-level competition. (6) Several factors are important to consider during this phase: (a) the physical well-being of the athlete should be assessed via a medical examination; (b) the athlete's training methods should be measured and modified to insure optimum physical preparation (this factor should be the primary responsibility of the coach); (c) psychological interviews and tests should be given to determine the degree to which the athlete is motivated to do well in the impending competitions, as in the cases where Olympic team members may not desire to extend themselves further because they have achieved their goals by merely "making the team" and do not aspire to win over their opponents in the impending contests.

During this period the psychologist and the coach should be sensitive to the manner in which the group dynamics of the team may evolve. As an example, when several athletes have been selected from a larger group for high-level competition, there may be an adjustment of friendships, leadership, and dependent roles and group motivations. The coach during this period should attempt to become cognizant of these and should try to engender cohesion in the newly formed social structure. Various sociometric tests administered by the psychologist during this period may aid the coach in evaluating these types of subtle group interactions and feelings.

During this period also there is a healthy level of fear of losing, which is desirable. Coaches should see that this fear is present, and that overconfidence is not prevalent among team members.

To summarize, the primary considerations during this first pre-performance period include the assessment of the motivational levels of athletes, evaluations, and accommodations to the social dynamics of the newly formed team, basic skill development, the improvement of strength and cardiovascular endurance as needed, and the physical health of the athlete.

THE PRE-START PERIOD. This second period, occurring a day or two prior to competition, is an extremely important one. In general, care must be taken that the athlete's tension curve does not "peak" too soon and that he has not passed the point of optimum activation.

Several physiological considerations with psychological ramifications are important during this pre-start period, just prior to competition. For example, at times athletes during this period may crave some kind of extra protein, vitamins, or the like. In general, if the athlete has followed a correct diet, these requests should be denied, as any marked change in diet may disrupt the athlete's physiological balance, which may elicit harmful effects during performance.

The athlete's sleep patterns should be carefully monitored during this period. It is not usually harmful if an athlete does not sleep well the night prior to competition, as indeed this may be normal in many athletes. If, however, it is apparent that the athlete will have difficulty sleeping several nights prior to competition, he should be administered sleeping pills. Care should be taken, however, that the sedatives do not produce a lethargy the following day. Prior to competition, the athlete should sleep from six to seven hours a night, and sedatives which induce sleep for longer periods of time should be avoided.

As there is generally a tapering off of training during these final days, the athlete will tend to have more free time available to him. Provision should be made for the constructive use of this time. A planned program of leisure activities, including entertainment, books, excursions, and the like, is sometimes helpful.

Care should be taken that leisure-time activity does not contain emotional overtones. For example, movies with a profound message or tragic endings might be avoided. Games in which there is a great deal of stress should be similarly kept to a minimum. The best leisure-time activities during this time are often provided by the athletes themselves, including informal singing, and the like. An assistant coach might initiate these kinds of activities in a natural rather than in a forceful way.

Self-rating scales obtained from athletes in Europe have revealed that successful participation in the types of leisure-time activities described above contribute positively to an athlete's emotional state prior to competition.

If it is found that an athlete evidences unusually high levels of tension activation, various relaxants may be administered by an attending physician. Often harmful excess tensions evidenced a few days prior to competition can be successfully adjusted in this way. If ignored, they may become too high for either the athlete or the coach to manage.

At times the coach may relax "high-strung" performers by directing their attention toward other matters. The impending competition might be avoided in conversation. At other times the coach may concentrate upon instilling self-confidence in the athletes by referring to their recent and successful performance efforts posted in practices.

In summary, during this pre-start period, a day or two prior to competition, attention should be paid to calming the performer, to filling up his free time so that he may not concern himself too much about the impending contest, his diet, or his sleep. Activation levels may be controlled by relaxants, by directing his attention away from himself and his impending performance, as well as by positive references to the athlete's good efforts in recently completed training sessions.

During this period and the post-tension period, athletes often exhibit varying degrees of sexual needs. Some feel that sexual intercourse prior to competition is necessary to their good performance, while others do not. In general, there is a greater variance in sexual needs prior to competition, with some athletes experiencing less sexual desire than normal, while others report feeling an increase of the sex drive. In general, following competition athletes usually report an increase in their sex drive, and will seek this and other forms of relaxation, particularly if they have experienced success in their endeavors on the athletic field.

In this period it is not unusual to see athletes engage in superstitious behaviors. They may enter the stadium in unique ways, or perhaps have some kind of doll accompany them. Generally, the coach should expect this and should attempt to tolerate this kind of behavior. Ridicule is usually not helpful to an athlete behaving in this manner.

START TENSION. Hours and minutes prior to competition when an athlete enters the performance environment, he experiences additional stress and tension. For many athletes some kind of warmup is important. While the physiological reasons for this type of activity have been debated, it is generally useful for psychological reasons. By pre-activity of this nature an athlete can often regulate his level of tension prior to the task he is to engage in.

If a team is preparing for competition, the warmup should generally consist of group effort first, and then each individual should be given an opportunity to warm up according to his own needs.

Some European psychologists contend that most athletes do not warm up enough to adjust their levels of activation to the optimum. Studies by Americans have indicated that in general warmup aids those who believe that warmup is important to perform better, while it does not aid those who express the opinion that warmup is of little importance.

Massage is often used by European athletic teams during this stage of preparation just prior to performance. Again the intensity and duration of the massage should be individualized and should relax and stimulate each athlete according to his needs.

Cold and hot showers can often be utilized to advantage during this warmup period. In this way the muscles can be warmed without the possibility of fatigue that may come about with the practice of extensive amounts of vigorous warmup exercises.

At times warmup activities, showers, massages, or exercises may be needed prior to competition, and at other times in other types of activities additional warmup may be needed between components of the competition. Field-event athletes, gymnasts, divers, and others who perform for short periods of time interspersed with rest periods may need additional activity to prepare themselves between "bouts."

In many team sports the substitutes often tend to spend too much time watching. It may be advisable in some cases to have the substitutes engage in vigorous activity when the others are in competition. Immobile spectator-substitutes often catch the emotional content of the sports situation without the opportunity to release it in movement. As a result the substitutes may be at too high a level of activation when they enter the game, unless some of this emotionality is released by vigorous warmup on the side lines.

It may be desirable during the time immediately before competition to keep individuals who have recently lost in competition away from individuals who are about to compete. The research literature is replete with studies outlining how one individual transfers his emotional state to adjacent individuals. Thus the negative feelings the loser has about the competitive situation may transfer to the current competitor in an undesirable way.

In addition to massage, warmup, and the like, many cultures and subcultures around the world have developed special ways of activating or deactivating the mind and body. Yoga is practiced in certain parts of India. Japanese Sumo wrestlers engage in contemplative activities prior to a bout, while in other countries hypnosis and self-hypnotic types of activities are engaged in in order to adjust the psychic states of individuals under immediate or long-term stresses of various kinds.

Edmund Jacobson, a physician in the United States, has developed what has been termed Progressive Relaxation, described in several texts written in 1938 and 1964. (2), (3) Generally, this technique involves aiding an individual to adjust his level of activation by helping him to become aware of residual muscular tensions he may be experiencing. The individual is taught to tighten and to relax various muscle groups to varying degrees, and in this way, it has been hypothesized, a number of physiological and physical problems may be reduced.

Many athletes find it helpful to pray in church and in this way reduce emotional tensions that may have occurred because of impending competition.

Many athletes in Europe, under the direction of several sport psychologists, have developed special means by which activation levels may be adjusted in rather specific ways.

This methodology has been termed "autogenic training" or "psychotonic training," depending upon the country in which it has been practiced. In general, the technique was formulated by J. H. Schultz and was described in his text titled *Das Autogenne Training* (The Self-Training). (12) This type of training, originally developed for psychotic patients, has been frequently found to be helpful during the period just prior to competition.

It has several uses with athletes. It can be used with individuals whose start tension is too high or too low. To either raise or lower levels of activation, the psychologist (or the athlete himself after two or three months' experience) begins in the following way. The athlete is placed in a comfortable position, usually lying on his back. It is suggested that he breathe deeply and concentrate upon his breath and its depth. He is asked to tighten all the muscles in his body as hard as he can, and then to relax as completely as possible. This alternating tightening and relaxing is executed three or more times.

Following this initial preparation, the athlete is asked to concentrate upon various body parts, and to attempt to make them as relaxed as possible. First he is asked to think about making one of his arms "as heavy as possible," so heavy, in fact, that it cannot be lifted. Then this is repeated with the other arm, with the legs (one at a time), and then with the abdominal and chest regions. This kind of suggestion relative to the relaxation of the limbs may be repeated several times until it is obvious that the athlete is totally relaxed. Furthermore, he is asked to ignore his environment and to concentrate upon himself, his body, and its parts. Sometimes the psychologist will lift a limb of the athlete and see whether it is relaxed or not by dropping it back on the floor, and observing whether it is lowered slowly by the athlete or whether it falls naturally of its own weight.

Following several minutes of this initial relaxation training (which in many ways resembles Jacobson's techniques to this point), it is then suggested to the athlete that first one limb and then the other is becoming warm, "as though it is in warm water." This is repeated several times, and other parts of the body are involved in this type of suggestion, i.e., the chest, neck, stomach, and so on, until the athlete experiences a feeling of warmth. Furthermore, it may be suggested that a "warm

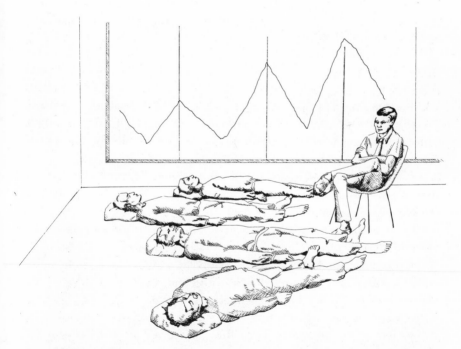

Figure 12. Athletes are shown engaging in Autogenne training under the supervision of a team psychologist. The chart in the background illustrates the manner in which various indices of activation level (blood pressure, heart rate, galvanic skin response, and so on) may be alternately lowered and raised using this type of training.

wave" is passing from the head to the feet, or in a reverse direction from the feet to the head.

At this point, if it is desired that the athlete sleep, he is often left alone, since he is usually almost asleep. If it is desired that he become activated to a level appropriate for competition, he is asked to again tighten his muscles and to imagine himself in the competition, i.e., "Imagine you are fighting and tighten your muscles hard." This is again repeated until it is determined by the observer that he is at an appropriate level of activation. It is believed that an athlete will return, after first relaxing to an appropriate level, in a more positive frame of mind, suitable for more effective performance.

In most of Europe, especially in Russia, Bulgaria, France, Germany, Hungary, and Poland, athletes, their trainers, and psychologists practice this method with their own unique variations. These variations occur in the manner in which the verbal suggestions are offered. Some variations occur in the beginning stages relative to the number of times the individual is asked to tighten his muscles, others may omit this tightening of the muscles altogether, and may proceed directly to the phase during which it is suggested that various body parts and the total body are warm.[2]

All athletes cannot practice this technique with positive outcomes. For example, the athlete must participate in this kind of psychotonic training voluntarily. The athlete should be reasonably intelligent; an I.Q. of over 100 is usually needed. The athlete should have the power to concentrate intensely, and must be reasonably suggestible. It has been found that about 40–45 per cent of all athletes can participate profitably in this type of activation adjustment.

After an introduction to this type of training with the help of a psychologist, it has been found that many athletes can successfully apply this method to themselves. With continued practice the athlete can usually shorten the amount of self-instruction, can omit phrases, can concentrate upon a word or two which will trigger desired feelings and, furthermore, can be expected to engage in this type of self-suggestion in a variety of environments, i.e., sitting in a chair, in a dressing room, or while sitting on a bench.

Although it is usual for athletes to practice this technique during

---

[2] The theory and practice of autogenic training was discussed in a special colloquium in Paris in May 1967 organized by Dr. Eric DeWinter. About seventy scholars were present at this meeting.

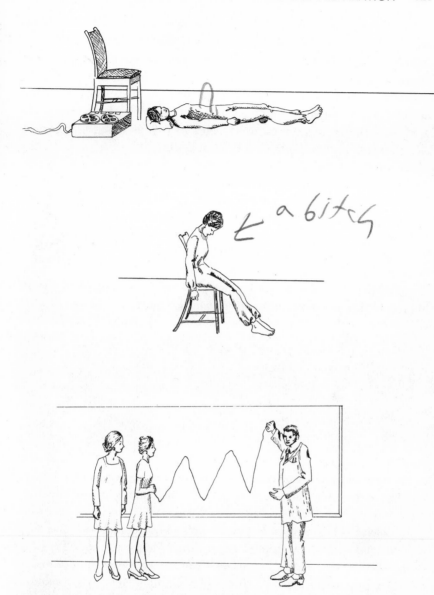

Figure 13. The illustrations depict variations in Autogenne training. The top picture shows an athlete attending to a tape recording of instructions. The middle picture illustrates this type of training being engaged in while sitting, and self-administered. The bottom picture indicates the manner in which athletes may be afforded constant "feedback" concerning their psychophysiological responses during sessions of this type of training.

specified hours of the day, its application should not be limited in this way. Whenever an athlete feels under stress, upset, or in other ways fearful of impending competition, he should be encouraged to engage in this autogenic training if he is able.

In Figure 14, the levels of activation reached on the vertical axis, indicated by the ascending white lines in the black blocks, have been evaluated by recording blood pressure changes, as well as changes in galvanic skin response, in one hundred and fifty subjects.

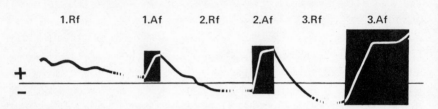

Figure 14. Activation levels reached after repeated applications of the Machak method of relaxation-activation training.

KEY:

1.Rf = 1st relaxation training phase
1.Af = 1st reactivation phase
2.Rf = 2nd relaxation phase
2.Af = 2nd reactivation phase
3.Rf = 3rd relaxation phase
3.Af = 3rd reactivation phase

The time on the horizontal axis indicates three periods of relaxation training lasting about fifteen minutes each. The periods of activation (the black blocks) last fifteen seconds each.

The chart indicates on a plus and minus horizontal line the changes in activation after three applications of the Machac method. The chart thus indicates that activation achieved following three applications of relaxation training is usually raised to levels higher than those achieved after only one application.

Machak (7), Professor of Psychology at Charles University, Prague, has developed what is termed a nonverbal variation of the Schultz method. In general, individuals are encouraged to imagine themselves in an environment which for them will induce relaxation, whether it be by the seashore, in a forest, or in some similar place. Activation is accomplished by combining short breaths with application of voluntary tension by various muscle groups.

Machak has investigated the manner in which various muscular and physiological processes are modified when individuals are practicing this kind of relaxation training. In general it has been found that (a) pulse rate can be significantly slowed below the usual resting rate of the individual; (b) muscle tension changes can be induced that are also below residual tension found usually within the individual's musculature; (c) at the termination of the activation phase, the individual's levels of muscle tension and physiological measures become higher than normally experienced and assessed; (d) adrenal changes persist after this kind of training for about twenty-four hours at abnormally high levels, and thus they are prepared hormonally for a high level of competition for a prolonged period of time; (e) via questionnaires, it was found that the individuals subjected to this method evidenced more positive responses relative to their readiness for action; (f) if the athlete is proficient in the method, it has been found that when one limb is imagined to be warmer than the other, real temperature differences amounting to from one to two degrees are often recorded when comparing the surface warmth of the two limbs.

Infrequently athletes have been hypnotized to purportedly raise performance levels via post-hypnotic suggestions. Publicity was given a few years ago to the Australian swimmers who were supposed to have been subjected to the post-hypnotic suggestion that "sharks were chasing them." However, the research shows and experience of sport psychologists in Europe substantiates the fact that helpful post-hypnotic suggestion can be applied to very few athletes and only in very general ways. One may, for example, lead an athlete to feel generally more aggressive, more relaxed, or perhaps more comfortable by way of a post-hypnotic suggestion. Experience shows, however, that specific suggestions are likely to be disruptive, and may well lead to rigid inflexible kinds of movements that are likely to be disruptive of good performance. Hypnosis does not permit an athlete to modify his exertions to an unexpected situation that may confront him, e.g., the challenge of an opponent in a race.

Furthermore, when working with superior athletes, it is usually found that they are often highly self-controlled individuals who are not only difficult or impossible to hypnotize, but who also want to take all the credit for their efforts. They resist any technique that would tend to place the accolades for their winning in the hands of another individual, i.e., the hypnotist. Thus it is believed that little promise may be held, with our present state of knowledge, for the use of hypnosis with top athletic performers.

Power and Lerner (8) have reported that positive improvement in teamwork on the part of a Brazilian soccer team was achieved due to post-hypnotic suggestions "to work better together." However, there is no way to substantiate the data accompanying their report involving measures of team cohesion.

The social contact occurring between the athlete and the coach is critical during this period of start tension immediately prior to competition. Not only verbal, but nonverbal communication occurring between the two is important. Many superior athletes like to be alone just prior to competition. They find that their level of concentration may be broken if demands are placed upon them to communicate to others, even to their coaches, during this period. Thus the coach should proceed with caution and carefully assess the individual needs of his athletes before he expects to communicate with them prior to the race, game, or competitive effort.

This critical period is usually not the time for the coach to extend complicated information to an athlete concerning strategy, technique, or the like. The stresses the athlete is under will usually not permit him to make any complicated changes in his behavior, despite the most well-meaning suggestions offered by his coach or by others.

Some performers may need some kind of general verbal suggestion in order to raise or to lower their level of activation. To cite two extreme cases, they may need to be told to "hate" their opponent, while on the other hand, an athlete may be told that winning or losing makes little difference. Most, however, require some kind of general verbal suggestion intermediate between these two extremes. It is, therefore, imperative that the coach be cognizant of the level of activation experienced by each of his charges, the activation demanded of each task, as well as the means by which he may best adjust his charge's activation levels to the optimum.

Thus during the start tension period the coach should not extend any complicated last-minute directions. At the same time, activation levels may be adjusted in some athletes by the specific relaxation-activation techniques described. Hypnosis is not recommended, especially if it involves some kind of detailed post-hypnotic suggestion. Furthermore, it is recommended that the athlete be left to himself without an excess of interference by coach or psychologist.

TENSION DURING COMPETITION. During competition, many events are not amenable to the adjustment of changes among their competitors. Short sprints and brief efforts of various kinds, of course, do not permit any kind of arousal changes to be induced from an outside source. In more prolonged games in which such tension changes can be effected, however, it is important to proceed with caution so that performance is not affected negatively. The coach and/or the team psychologist should attempt to adjust tensions with care in these latter types of activities, and only when they are thoroughly familiar with the athletes with whom they are working.

POST-PERFORMANCE TENSION. Post-task tension is usually related to, and indeed overlaps, long-term pre-task tension for future competitions. A kind of feedback mechanism occurs from one competitive effort to the next; thus proper management of post-task tensions is vital.

It has already been mentioned that several kinds of aggression, euphoria, and/or some kind of depression may occur after a contest. It is best, therefore, that individuals not connected directly with the team be kept out of contact with the athletes. The losers do not need to be reminded of this fact, while at the same time the winners usually do not need all the attention usually afforded them.

It is important that the coach define the meaning of the win or loss to the athletes following competition. A loss is not necessarily an unsuccessful effort, and should be correctly interpreted by the coach.

Care must be taken to attempt to understand individual levels of frustration, aggression, and/or euphoria experienced by various individuals who have just won or lost. Each player will interpret his unique role and responsibility for winning or losing in different ways. It is important that the coach realize this and act accordingly. Thus it may be important to speak to several players individually in order to help them to correctly interpret their own efforts, and to point out the ways in which success or lack of success is related to, or independent of, winning or losing.

Interpretation of a group's success or failure or of an individual's success or failure, of course, should be carried out with regard to their/ his background of experience. More experienced expert athletes should have more demanded of them and should not be led to think of losing as necessarily a successful experience. Less experienced younger athletes, on the other hand, may be encouraged to believe that even a losing effort may be successful!

There are sometimes sexual differences in the manner in which winning and losing are interpreted. It is often found that women have less tolerance for losing and often engage in intra-punitive behavior (self-blame) following a loss. There are often paradoxical reactions among top women athletes when winning and losing. When they win, they often weep; when they lose, they often smile.

Relaxation after competition may be induced in a number of ways. Athletes may be permitted an extended period of time by themselves, in the showers, for example, prior to being interrupted or stimulated by the presence of the coach. Following this period the coach may in general terms offer his interpretation of an individual's performance. The time for more objective and pointed criticism is usually the next day, when the athletes have had time to rest, to relax, and to assess their own performance in precise terms.

For the mental health of the team, the coach should attend more to the unsuccessful athlete than to the successful ones immediately following the game or contest. To the performer of this type, he should offer the chance of future success. On the other hand, the coach should be sensitive to the "prima donna" effect among his more successful athletes, and help such individuals to place their performance in proper perspective.

The day following the contest, the coach should cover in detail mistakes and positive reactions made by individuals and by the team on the previous day. On some European teams, relaxants are sometimes administered following the game to prevent an excess of anxiety-producing and fatiguing "rehashing" of the game far into the night. Other types of relaxing activities may also be engaged in following the game, such as recreation of various types and other social activities that are helpful in reducing the sometimes marked amount of post-task tension experienced by athletes. The Schultz method can also be employed.

Thus, following competition the coach should first permit the athletes to get out of contact with the competitive situation, and then should in general ways bolster those who might feel that their performance contributed to a loss. After a "cooling-off" period of a day, the coach should carefully interpret the relative success or failure of their group or individual efforts, regardless of whether a win or a loss has been incurred.

A number of activities may be utilized to reduce the great amount of pre-performance tension experienced by athletes. These include participation in recreational activities of various kinds, taking various relaxants, and the like. Individuals who may either be overly elated upon winning and upon surveying their own efforts as well as players who may be engaging in unusual amounts of intra-punitive aggression need the coach's special attention following a contest.

REFERENCES

1. Brustmann, M. "Start Fieber" (Start Fever). *Zeitschrift der Sex. Wissenschaft*, 16–22, 1923.
2. Jacobson, Edmund. *Anxiety and Tension Control*. Philadelphia: J. B. Lippincott, 1964.
3. Jacobson, Edmund. *Progressive Relaxation*. Chicago: University of Chicago Press, 1938 (revised edition).
4. Krestovnikov, A. N. *Narys Fyziologie Telesnych Cviceni* (The Outline of the Physiology of Physical Exercises). Prague, 1954.
5. Lechtmann, J. B. *Analiz Startovovo Sostojania* (Analyses of the Start Tension). Leningrad, 1942.
6. Macak, I. *Psychologia Sportu* (Sports Psychology). Bratislava: Sport Publisher, 1962.
7. Machak, M. "Relaxacne-Aktivacni, Autoregulacni Zasah. Metoda Nacviku a Psychologicka Charakterestika" (The Relaxation-Activation, Self-Regulative Action. The Method of Training and the Psychological Characteristic). *Csl. Psychologie* (Czechoslovakian Psychology), 3, 1964.
8. Power, E., and Lerner, M. "Hipnosis v Deporte" (Hypnosis and Sports Activity). *Rev. Del Derechno Deportivo*, 1961, 2.
9. Puni, A. C. "K Psichologiceskoj Charakteristiki Predstartovnych Sostojanij Sportsmena" (Psychological Characteristics of Pre-Start Tensions of Athletes). *Teoriya i Praktika Fiz. Kultury*, Moscow, 7, 1949.
10. Puni, A. C. "Nektere Otazky Psychologicke Pripravy Sportovce" (Some Questions Concerning the Psychological Preparation of the Athlete). *Teorie a Praxe Telesne Vychovy*, Prague, 7, 1962.
11. Roudik, P. A., and Puni, A. C. *Psichologiceskaja Podgotovka Sportsmena* (The Psychological Preparation of the Athlete). Moscow: Fizkultura i Sport, 1965.
12. Schultz, J. H. *Das Autogenne Training. Konzentrative Selbstentspannung* (The Self-Training. The Concentrative Self-Relaxation). Stuttgart, 1956.

13. Tschernikova, O. A. *Emocii v Sporte* (Emotions in Sports Activity). Moscow, 1962.
14. Vanek, M. "Teorie Psychologicke Pripravy Sportovce" (The Theory of the Psychological Preparation of the Athlete). *Dissertation*, Philosophical Faculty, University of Charles, Prague, 1964.
15. Vanek, M. "Vliv Startovnich Stavu na Pohybovou Koordinaci" (The Influence of Start-Tensions upon the Movement Coordination). Volume of Scientific Works of the Faculty of Physical Education, Prague, 1965.
16. Vasiljeva, V. V. "Startove Rozpolozenie Sportovce vo Svetle Uceni I. P. Pavlova" (The Start-Tension of the Athlete in the Light of the Pavlov Theory). *Sokol*, 1, 1951.

CHAPTER 8

Model Training

The bases of so-called "model training" have been derived from the theory of homeostasis and from Selye's theory of adaptation to stress. (1) The material on the pages that follow was arrived at after continually observing vast differences in the psychological stresses to which athletes are subjected in training when contrasted with the stresses to which they are exposed in actual competitive situations.

During training for competition, psychological stress upon athletes is usually minimal; however, during competitive efforts, there is more emotional pressure exerted upon the performer. Normally an athlete trains without any special training for the competitive second part of the dyad. At the same time, competition itself is a form of training, for when an athlete competes, he learns to perform under stress, to control his emotions, to raise his tension and arousal levels to an optimum level befitting the conditions he is facing.

To an increasing degree coaches throughout the world, realizing that competitive performances are stressful, are attempting to insert into practice sessions the variables which impinge upon the athlete during competition. Vanek has termed this "model training," that is, training which delineates the competitive environments that the athlete will later face. (2), (3) Essentially this model training involves inserting some combination of social, psychological, and technical stresses into the training situation in order to more closely duplicate the conditions the athlete will later meet when contested by an opponent. Specific training under conditions duplicating those he will later meet should accelerate his adaptations to competition and should facilitate his performance efforts under competitive circumstances.

For example, when track athletes are engaged in interval training, they learn to run, rest; run, rest in given intervals and to adapt to given intensities that are applied in a rather rhythmical manner. However, during a race, one's opponent usually imposes rather unexpected stresses in the form of challenges at irregular and unpredictable times. It would therefore be better, when engaging in interval training, to keep the intensity high while at the same time trying to duplicate these unpredictable demands made upon the athlete during training. He may, for example, be asked to sprint suddenly within the second of a series of paced 400-meter runs which he had originally planned to run at only three-fourth speed. The sudden imposition of unexpected stress combined with the physical demands thus duplicates the emotional conditions that will usually be encountered in competition. Thus, exposure to this type of training should hasten adaptation to the physical as well as to the emotional stresses of competitive distance or middle-distance running.

Another example of the imposition of psychological and physical stress that is possible during practice sessions is as follows: Many athletes are unaware of how it really feels to extend themselves fully in an all-out performance. They tend to run, swim, walk, or work well "within themselves." Coaches of such athletes could at infrequent times in the season during practice suddenly ask the individual to extend himself at the end of a so-called "all-out performance." If he is running an 800-meter race, at what is purportedly his best time, he may be asked, just as he nears the end of the race, to "run fifty or seventy-five yards farther." This method should result in an athlete gaining a feeling of overload and of the pain incurred of extending performance limits in taxing endurance tasks. At the same time this technique should also aid the athlete to adapt to the pain and emotional stress endured when experiencing this type of overload. It is true, of course, that this kind of "game" cannot be "played" too often on athletes; however, it is believed that if carried out about once a week, helpful adaptations to the competitive situation will occur.

Technical stresses can also be imposed on the athlete that may aid him to adapt to the emotional climate of competition. For example, in volleyball service practice or in basketball shooting practice it is common to see an athlete execute a given type of shot or serve many times in succession. In opposition to this would be the kind of technical stress imposed on this shooting or serving practice in which the coach demanded that the player practice fewer but more perfect efforts.

This kind of "technical" stress may also take the form of requiring the athlete to unexpectedly shoot a given type of shot, or to serve to a given point on the court with a given type of serve in volleyball at irregular intervals. For example, the coach may in a random and unpredictable order call for one of five kinds of basketball shots that the athlete is required to respond to at his best technical level. Research from a number of studies has demonstrated quite clearly that the axiom "practice makes perfect" is rather inexact and at times naïve. One should be concerned with the quality of practice and in athletes, particularly, the quality of physical performance obtained under conditions which involve some kind of emotional stress.

It is common to see coaches impose what might be termed "tactical" stresses during practice. The shooting characteristics of a team they are to play are duplicated by the reserves in a basketball practice. The starting players will thus become accustomed to seeing given types of shots being taken from a given portion of the floor and thus be more adaptable when actually meeting the team that has been modeled in the competitive situation. Football teams frequently practice against "mock-ups" of their opponents for a week or more prior to meeting the actual team. Members of the reserve squads often adopt the performance characteristics of key players on the opposing team.

Athletes may also be trained to accommodate to the stress of audience reactions. European sports psychologists have frequently recommended to coaches that using loud-speaker systems broadcasting crowd reactions during practice is likely to better prepare the teams for competition under the same distracting and stressful circumstances. Coaches who have followed this advice report that their teams did seem less susceptible to the distraction and pressure exerted by friendly and unfriendly crowd noises. Although experimental evidence concerning the validity of this technique is lacking, the opportunity to verify its worth should not be overlooked for long by enterprising graduate students.

Various kinds of handicapped training can also be imposed during practices for competition. This type of handicapping can be among two or more individuals running a race or swimming, or can be imposed between two teams. A runner who is behind often does not try to catch up, for he feels that it is impossible. However, if he is given "catching-up" training in practice sessions, he may be more likely to persevere in competition. Similarly, a swimmer who is leading in a race often does not realize that he can be surpassed; thus when conducting practice sessions, the coach may stage "races" in which the athletes are placed at various intervals relative to each other within a race and asked to see who can pass whom before the termination of the contest.

This type of handicapping, of course, can be used in team situations. Toward the end of a basketball practice one of the two teams can be informed that they are now four points behind with only three minutes to go and be encouraged to catch up while the other team is encouraged to "protect their lead." Football teams in America often practice "running out the clock" with side-line passes, incompletions, and attempts to gain a maximum number of yards within the shortest time interval.

Athletes often experience feelings of isolation when they engage in high-level competition. At times these feelings are justified, for it is not uncommon to find that athletes proceed to higher competition without their usual coaches, or without any coach at all. The boy from the remote high school may make the state finals in track, the college man may become a member of the Olympic team and perform under a coach he has known for only a few weeks. It is thus suggested that a coach engage in what might be termed "independence training" with his athletes, particularly when he can foresee that one or more of his players may find himself isolated from him at a later date. For example, the high school senior may be asked to prepare his own workout for a week, and/or the coach will tell him that he will not speak to him for several days before the next competition or during the day of competition. Preparing the athlete to "fend for himself" in this manner should result in his experiencing less psychological discomfort in later contests when he may be out of contact with his familiar coach or trainer.

These modifications of what has been termed "model training" are based upon valid theories of stress, adaptation, and learning. Although many of these practices have been used successfully by coaches both in America and in Europe during the past several decades, their validity has not been verified by any significant number of well-controlled experiments.

One must proceed with caution when applying some of these principles of model training to the less experienced athletes. Unexpected stresses of the kind described if imposed in training upon the less adroit could prove devastating. At the same time the imposition of some of the stresses outlined in the previous pages should hasten the superior athlete's adaptation to competitive circumstances. This type of model training should not be used in excess, as it is possible that it will over-stress even superior athletes. It may, however, be employed to advantage as an integral part of the training regime of superior athletes in most sports.

Essentially the coach should attempt to duplicate the technical, tac-tical, psychological, social, and situational stresses of competition prior to competition so that athletes may adapt, change, and thus improve their individual and group performance. Model training of the types described thus involves the insertion of a helpful emotional dimension to sports practice that in the past has often only involved some kind of mechanical acquisition of skills.

REFERENCES

1. Selye, Hans. *The Stress of Life*. New York: McGraw-Hill, 1956.
2. Vanek, Miroslav. "L'Entrainement Modele" (Model Training). *Proceedings, First International Congress of Sports Psychology*, F. Antonelli (ed.), Rome, 1965.
3. Vanek, Miroslav. "La Preparation Psychologique" (The Psychological Prepa-ration of the Athlete). *Proceedings* of Sport Sciences Conference, Tokyo, 1964.

CHAPTER 9

Intellectual Training of the Athlete

While statistical studies in which intelligence has been correlated to various performance measures often provide contradictory findings, it would seem that with further research it might be possible to isolate kinds of intelligence which enable some individuals to perform well in a variety of motor skills. Some speak of the ability to engage in efficient motor planning or, as Seashore has written, the adoption of sound work methods that may be generalized from activity to activity. (6) Several types of findings have emerged upon investigating intellectual performance relationships among and between groups of athletes in Europe and in the United States.

1. In general, superior athletes possess average and above average I.Q.'s. For example, in a recent study of the intelligence levels of superior athletes in Czechoslovakia their average I.Q. was found to be 118 (S.D. 11.3). The Ravens test, previously described, was used in this investigation. (2)

2. It is probable that the more information extended to an athlete about the physiological, psychological, and mechanical demands of the sport he is engaging in, the more likely it is that he will excel. (5)

3. There are probably several specific kinds of intellectual attributes necessary in the proficient performance of a given sports activity.

Studies of athletes in Europe have revealed that in general higher socioeconomic groups composed of university students are likely to gravitate more toward team sports; and thus within groups of athletes engaged in basketball, volleyball, and handball there is more likely to be found a preponderance of higher I.Q. scores. On the other hand, individuals from less advantaged backgrounds are more likely to gravitate toward combative sports, such as wrestling, boxing, and the like, and as a group tend to post lower intelligence scores. It is difficult, of course, to determine whether the I.Q. measures obtained in the two groups are a reflection of the participants' backgrounds, their innate intelligence, or of more subtle factors.

Athletes selecting, and excelling in, track and field, on the other hand, are likely to be composed of individuals from either part of the social scale, and when I.Q. scores are averaged, they are likely to fall midway between those of the boxers and wrestlers and the athletes participating in team sports.

Investigations of athletes at several levels of proficiency have explored the influence of special training in sports mechanics, physiology, and psychological problems on physical activity as reflected in performance scores. Kozlik, for example, utilizing four hundred high school age boys, inserted into the program for an experimental group special intellectual training concerning the values of physical activity. He found that superior performance was indeed recorded after a year of this type of special tutoring. (4) This was compared to a control group who received no special attention and who were exposed only to the physical demands of the tasks. The experimental group's attitudes as well as their performance and fitness levels were significantly better than the controls.

Intellectual training may take several forms and concern various topics. It may be carried out in connection with training, prior to extensive training, or it may be interpolated between practice sessions. In Russia, Poland, Hungary, Romania, Czechoslovakia, and East Germany it is becoming common practice to expose superior athletes to the theory and mechanics of their sport. (9)

At times coaches assign readings to their athletes, while at other times discussions are held and lectures are given by authorities who are invited to discuss the psychological or physiological ramifications of the activity in which the athletes are engaged. These training sessions frequently expose the athlete to training films in which their own movements are analyzed and compared to those of more proficient performers from around the world.

Team sportsmen may engage in extensive discussion of tactics. As in America, special training aids may be used; for example, tactics may be demonstrated on chalkboards and boards where simulated players may be moved and discussed. Players must verbalize and take tests concerning the tactics they should display in given situations as a check on the retention of the material presented.

Recent speculation by several Russian and Czechoslovakian psychologists concerning intellectual processes prior to and during competition provides a possible impetus for further investigations. (1), (6), (3) They suggest, for example, that during competition an athlete thinks in visual images, rather than in words; while following competition the athlete may be able to verbalize about his performance. Thus it is suggested that two types of thought processes may be involved—one in which visual imagery is more pronounced, and a second in which word cues are chained together to describe the movement. Vanek's thoughts on this subject should also be accorded careful attention, as athletes and coaches often experience or observe the manner in which an overemphasis upon word cues during the performance of a movement may result in "intellectual paralysis."

When an athlete does verbalize, it is likely that (a) it must be carried out rapidly, and (b) it is likely to be disrupted by overarousal, while at the same time verbal rehearsal after or before the task under conditions of optimum arousal will likely facilitate the analysis and/or acquisition of the desired skill. Further research should substantiate or negate these assumptions.

In summary, it has been found helpful to prepare athletes intellectually for the demands of the competitions they are to face. This type of preparation may take the form of discussions, lectures, and readings about the physiological, psychological, and biomechanical demands of the sport in which they are participating. While the value of this kind of training is being exploited by many coaches, there are still those who tend to resist this kind of preparation. As further insights are obtained concerning how to provide athletes with knowledge about the functioning of their own bodies, their psychological state, the mechanics of movements, and of group dynamics, even more superior performances are likely to be achieved.

Coaches who continue to drill athletes as animals, without explaining the whys of their practice demands, may encourage an overdependence by their athletes and at the same time are probably failing to elicit the best possible performances from their charges. It might be speculated that coaches of this type are in truth exposing their own distorted needs for authority and control rather than being truly concerned for the psychological and physical welfare of their athletes.

REFERENCES

1. Gagajeva, G. M. "Takticeskije Myslenie v Sporte" (Tactical Thinking in Sports Activity). *Teor. Praktika Fiz. Kult.*, 6, 1951.
2. Hosek, V. "Zjistovani Nekterych Vlastnosti Osobnosti u Sportovcu" (An Investigation of Some Personality Traits of Athletes). *Teorie a Praxe Telesne Vychovy*, Prague, **13**:1, 1965.
3. Choutka, M. "Nekotoryje Voprosy Takticeskoj Podgotovsky Futbalistov" (Some Questions on the Tactical Preparation of Soccer Players), *Mezdu Narodnaja Naucno-Metodiceskaja Konferencija po Problemam Sportivnoj Trenirouk* (The International Methodological Conference on the Problems of Sports Training), Moscow, 1962, II.
4. Kozlik, J. *Efektivita Vyucovaciho Procesv v Telesne Vychove* (The Efficiency Teaching of Physical Education). Prague: State Pedagogical Publisher, 1960.
5. Roudik, P. A. "Psichologiceskaja Podgotovka i Nravstnennoje Vospitanije Sportsmenov" (The Psychological Preparation and the Moral Development of Athletes). *Mezdunarodnaja Naucno-Metodiceskaja Konferencija Po Problemam Sportivnoj Trenirovki* (The International Scientific Methodological Conference on the Problems of Sports Training), Moscow, 1962, I.
6. Seashore, R. H. "Work Methods: An Often Neglected Factor Underlying Individual Differences." *Psych. Rev.*, **46**:123–41, 1939.
7. Svoboda, B. "Takticke Mysleni Hracu v Kosikove" (Tactical Thinking of Basketball Players). *Teorie a Praxe Telesne Vychovy*, Prague, 1, 1965.
8. Tschernikowa, O. A. *Psichologiceskaja Charakteristika Igry v Tennis* (Psychological Characteristics of Tennis). Moscow, 1958.
9. *Proceedings of the International Scientific Methods Conference on the Problems of Sports Training*, I, II, III, Moscow, 1962.

CHAPTER 10

Social-Psychological Preparation of Athletes

In team sports it is often found that simply grouping the best performers together may not elicit the best group performance. Rather, *preferably* for the more effective team effort, individuals who can interact well with each other's movements and moods should be selected. When a member of a national team is suddenly selected for Olympic competition, for example, it is often difficult to allow for and engender good group effort, as he is likely to be selected on the basis of individual excellence rather than the manner in which he interacts with another performer or performers. (5)

To overcome this problem, the Russian ice hockey team, for example, practices together for several years in preparation for international competition. The quality of their group effort is obvious upon viewing their performance in Grenoble and in Innsbruck. This kind of team training is intensified just prior to Olympic games by many other teams in Europe.

The Czechoslovakian handball team has been prepared in a similar manner. Brought together to training camps many weeks before encountering international competition, their practice together seems to engender success due to the quality of their interactions on the courts.

It is not always feasible to bring individuals together well in advance of high-level competitions; therefore, it is sometimes helpful to assess the social attributes and the quality of interactions of individuals who may compose recently formed teams. A sensitive coach can sometimes "feel" the nature of the group tensions, yet at the same time more formal evaluations may either confirm, refute, or at times offer deeper insights into the quality of group processes, than is possible by short-term observation by a coach or trainer.

In 1966, for example, a sociometric test was given to one team within a national team preparing for the 1968 Olympics, and it was found that two individuals with high needs for domination were likely to interact in a destructive manner when competing. This team of cyclists was composed of men whose abilities were likely to culminate in world record performance if some kind of social impairment had not shown itself.[1] As competition approached, it became evident that the presence of these two dominating cyclists would result in less rapid over-all performance than if one was substituted for, resulting in a team composed of three submissive and one domineering athlete.

On the recommendation of the team psychologist plus the intervention of a slight injury, this substitution was made, and the four remaining cyclists (now composed of one dominant and three submissive riders) performed well enough to win a world championship in the pre-Olympic games in Mexico City in 1966.

In a national ice hockey team a similar situation arose. A coalition had formed between two defense men, who were brothers, so that they formed an intense dislike for the third defense man. The sociogram indicated the presence of this coalition, and as a result the positions were rearranged in order to form a more harmonious sports team.

Generally intra-team conflicts of this nature are not as intense. However, when a team does begin to lose, the type of conflict described can cause a problem of large proportions.

Macak has attempted to plot sociometric relationships by observing and counting the number of direct interactions between players while they actually play the game. (1) For example, a count is kept of the number of times player B passes to player C, as contrasted to the number of times player B passes the ball to player D. Data of this kind seems to be predictive of the manner in which these same players indicate preferences on the usual sociogram obtained by graphing players as first and second friend choices. These studies are still in the exploratory

---

[1] Success in this event is based upon total speed achieved by each of four cyclists riding together, in which each takes a turn leading the group and "breaking" the wind.

stage, and further evidence of this nature should shed important light upon the social interactions and feelings between athletes engaged in highly competitive team sports.

Figure 15. Observers are shown carefully plotting the manner in which team members interact with each other during a game. These interactions (i.e., times they throw the ball to each of their teammates) are plotted and compared to sociograms composed of team member preferences for their teammates (i.e., most liked and least liked). Analysis of these comparisons often suggests the manner in which friendships or lack of rapport between team members is facilitating or impeding team play. Sociograms contributed by the coach of the team are also employed in these comparisons at times. From seven to eight observers have been assigned to teams for the entire seasons in these types of studies.

At times, even if a coach becomes aware of intra-group conflicts, he may be unable to adjust the team membership or the position played by the various athletes. Thus this kind of information may be used to aid in the resolution of intra-group conflicts via psychological interviews, including the confrontation of the players, and at times their coach.

Comparisons are sometimes made between sociograms formulated by the coach and a sociogram graphing friends obtained from player responses of their least and best liked team members. (2) Similar to the findings of studies of leadership carried on in the United States, it has been found that the more successful coaches are those who are more sensitive to the quality and nature of the group interactions and feelings and who are able to produce a sociogram which closely corresponds to the one graphed by recording player responses.

There are a number of ways in which improved understanding and compatibility has been achieved using sociometric data of members of highly skilled teams in Europe. Basically it is attempted to achieve balance between the amount of competition evidenced between team members as opposed to the cooperative behavior they may display. Thus the creation of an optimum level of group concordance is attempted. The better teams seem to be made up of individuals whose needs for success and individual achievement are relatively equal.

To maintain this level of optimum collaboration, the coach should attempt to criticize each member fairly and, when possible, to give each individual on the team equal opportunity to score, to participate, and to make the starting team. At times special games for reserve teams, if arranged, can contribute significantly to group morale.

Intra-group conflicts may be resolved in a number of ways. For example, the coach may speak to an individual or to the group about the group tensions he perceives.

Another interesting technique that has been employed with much success involves the use of a psychodrama. One form this may take is a one-to-one dialogue, in which the psychologist takes the role of the "devil's advocate" and with gentle and at times more explicit verbal harassment or encouragement attempts to uncover the athlete's deepest motives and feelings about life, his family, sports, team members, and the impending competition.

Another type of psychodrama may involve two or more athletes, led by a psychologist, who encourages them to act out their feelings and conflicts. Following such a dialogue, the participants are usually encouraged to reverse roles and to act the parts of their partners in the psychodrama.

The initial psychodrama in which a team engages must be carefully handled, and usually poses the most difficulty. Generally, it is best to carry it out in an environment with which the coach and athletes are familiar.

Group psychodramas are also employed on occasion. For example, a conflict between coaches and players may be dramatized. This may initially take the form of a discussion between the coach and his players. Following this initial phase, one of the team members may take the role of the coach, while the coach assumes the role of the athletes in his charge.

The value of the psychodrama is that it exposes conflicts and tends to "ventilate" feelings. If the psychodrama is properly led by a skilled psychologist, this exposure and discussion of conflicts tends to reduce them. However, there is inherent danger in this type of group therapy if it is not properly handled. An inexperienced coach may, if he attempts to construct a psychodrama without professional assistance, cause more conflicts than he resolves. The psychodrama may also be employed with athletes engaged in individual sports, for in such situations the athlete lives with others prior to competition and interacts with them in indirect ways during competition.

When research is carried out evaluating the results of this interesting technique more objectively, further refinements and more exact guidelines will probably be formulated.

In addition to the use of the psychodrama, various kinds of structured group discussions are often employed to aid in the resolution of social problems and in heightening the social and individual efficiency of individuals on athletic teams. These discussions, during which the team's interactions, attitudes, and group aspirations are discussed and evaluated along with the discussions of tactics, may take place before or after competition. (4)

Meetings before competition may discuss the nature, structure, and reasons behind the training regimes instituted. Meetings after competition, of course, would be more likely to consist of positive and negative evaluations of individuals and of teams. These discussions should result in positive criticisms to elicit future improvements.

At times during such meetings the coach may administer a questionnaire that the athlete does not have to sign. This questionnaire may assess feelings about the coach, team members, competition, the level of aspiration, and similar subjects. Such a questionnaire should be well prepared and should contain not only structured questions to which yes-no answers might be given, but also open-ended questions after which the athlete may be encouraged to explain his feelings in some detail.

Social programs that include the wife, girl friends, and children of athletes may similarly contribute to more effective team feelings. An athlete in training has severe impositions made on his time, and as a result he is taken away from his family for an inordinate amount of time. Social occasions of the type described may aid him to train harder and with a more positive attitude than when he is separated from his family for brief or extended periods.

The coach may relate to the athlete's family further by taking special pains to send letters and small gifts to the wives (equal gifts). In a similar way an effort on the part of the coach should be made to include the athlete's children in any event or in any trip that they can make comfortably.

Team members and coaches should be cognizant of the manner in which their roles differ, and of the type of appropriate behavior they may exhibit. (3) Similar to traditional studies of leadership, three general types of coaches—the authoritarian, the democratic coach, and the adviser—have been identified by Svoboda and Stransky, and by other European researchers. (4)

The "authoritarian coach" concentrates more upon the imposition of discipline. He functions like a dictator, and must therefore accept most of the blame if the team is unsuccessful.

The "democratic coach" functions as a confidant and a friend, offering suggestions and encouraging self-discipline.

The "adviser coach" offers frequent advice and help and often encourages an excess of dependent behavior on the part of his athletes.

Preliminary data on this question seems to indicate that the more successful coaches are those who have adopted a democratic approach and yet at the same time behave in a flexible manner, exerting authority when needed and extending advice when it is appropriate to team members who may need it.

However, the type of male "coaching personalities" most likely to work effectively with members of women's teams are the authoritarian type or the adviser type. The male coach who tends to become too permissive and who acts as a confidant and friend to members of a woman's team may encourage favoritism on the part of some participants and create an unhealthy situation in which personal attraction to one or more members may interfere with his effectiveness in handling the total group. If a real and honest attachment is formed between a coach and a woman athlete, it should be known to all and should not be carried out surreptitiously.

Since the traditional male role in society is generally a dominant one, the authoritarian personality may be a role with which women are reasonably comfortable. At the same time the emotionality of women may require that a coach of this type "unbend" and act as an adviser when they confront him with personal problems.

Little is known concerning the manner in which athletes assume various roles when participating in sports. Though further research is needed in this area, there are some preliminary observations which are important to consider. For example, it is apparent that the team captain may achieve his role in several ways, that is, he may be appointed by the coach or elected by the players. It is obvious that the latter way will lend more prestige to his attempts at leadership.

Frequently there is an unofficial captain, who has earned his leadership role through sound leadership behavior and competency, while at the same time there is an appointed captain, who is a different individual. The coach and others connected with the team should be aware of the potential conflicts in such a situation and should try to rectify them.

Other intra-personal conflicts may arise when the more experienced players are confronted with the less experienced younger ones. The older players usually form a closely knit social group that younger players may have difficulty entering. The coach should be sensitive to this problem on his team. If the younger players are not made to feel part of some group within the team, personal conflicts may arise relative to feelings of rejection and isolation.

This kind of in-group structure reveals itself in sociometric tests, in the manner in which they choose rooms and seating when traveling, as well as in the manner in which they interact when actually engaged in competition. It is, therefore, at times helpful to arrange seating and living accommodations so that the newer players are confronted with the older members of the team. A number of research studies indicate that friends are chosen on the basis of physical proximity and, conversely, that friends once established tend to seek each other's company. If at times this kind of natural grouping is disrupted artificially, it will often be found that new friendships will arise that will tend to strengthen bonds between older and younger players, a situation that is potentially healthy to the efficiency of the team.

At times the entrance of a new team member may be specifically prepared for, that is, by first explaining to the older members the nature of his role on the team and the type of individual he is. The newcomers should similarly be prepared by the coach by being cautioned not to exhibit too much pride in their presence. The coach may also ease a newcomer into the team situation by being careful to offer similar treatment to both new and older members in all situations. If this kind of preparation is not carried out, at times the newcomer will be abused and will be asked to subordinate himself to the older players and to render services which may be psychologically oppressive.

Summary

A number of obvious and subtle steps may be taken to enhance the psychological and social "health" of an athletic team. If properly led, various kinds of psychodramas may be engaged in to reduce group tensions and conflicts. Sociograms plotted during team play (based upon the number of obvious "motor" interactions) may be compared with more structured sociograms prepared by consulting players' friendship responses and/or by those of the coach or captain. Identification of group conflicts is often made easier by anticipating them prior to their occurring. Easing a new member into a team situation and/or preparing a group of experienced players to accept a younger player in obvious ways should resolve possible inter-personal conflicts.

REFERENCES

1. Macak, I. "Niektere Moznosti Psychologie v Sucasnem Rozvoji Teorie Telesne Vychovy" (Some Possibilities of Psychology in the Contemporary Development of the Theory of Physical Education). *Teorie a Praxe Telesne Vychovy*, **10**:11, 1962.
2. Petrak, B. "Cleneni a Zmeny Sportovnich Skupin" (The Structure and Dynamics of Sports Groups), in *Psychologicka Priprava Sportovce* (Psychological Preparation of the Athlete), Vanek, M. (ed.). Prague: Scientific Council of the Czechoslovakian Committee of Physical Education, 1964.
3. Svoboda, B. "Pokus o Urceni Socialnich Hracskych Typu" (An Attempt to Establish Social Types of Players). *Teorie a Praxe Telesne Vychovy*, Prague, **12**:12, 1964.
4. Svoboda, B., and Stransky, A. "Psychologicke Pusobeni Trenera" (The Psychological Influence of the Coach), in *Theoretical Bases of Psychological Preparation of the Athlete*, Vanek, M. (ed.). Prague: Scientific Council of the Czechoslovakian Committee of Physical Education, 1967.

5. Vanek, M., and Hosek, M. "El Caracter Especifico de las Relaciones Per-
sonales Entre los Miembros de Equipos Nacionales" (The Special Character
of the Relationship of the Members of the National Teams). *Ap. Med. Dep.*,
III, 2, 1966.

group discussions
1 example of psych.

IV

CLINICAL
APPLICATIONS

ONE OF the more important outcomes of experimental studies concentrating on the athlete and research dealing with the motor behavior and motor learning takes the form of clinical efforts to improve performance in high-level competitors. The material in this fourth section contains a description of the day-to-day and month-to-month efforts during a period of three years by the psychologist attached to the Czechoslovakian Olympic team when dealing with the problems of the superior athletes in his charge.

As will be noted upon reviewing the pages that follow, his procedures are the result of a synthesis of clinical techniques and of experimental findings. His successes and failures depended upon the degree to which he was able to accurately evaluate the motives, feelings, and capabilities of the athletes with whom he was associated. His efforts to assess and at times to modify the dynamics of the various sports groups are also chronicled.

Perhaps the reader will be impressed with the thorough ways in which the psychologist and team physicians surveyed the athletes assigned to them. It should also be illuminating to note the period of time during which the team was measured and analyzed by the scientists who accompanied them to three countries and to several climatic environments.

It will be of further interest to note the manner in which the behavioral scientist and physiologists attempted in all ways and at all times to be of as much practical help as was possible. The frequent conferences with the coaches and with the athletes themselves attest to the real effort made by the evaluators to be constructive in their efforts. The scientists attempted to elicit optimum performance from over one hundred and thirty athletes at a given place and at a prescribed time—a feat whose difficulty was added to by the innumerable personal, climatic, political, social, and cultural variables permeating the complex atmosphere in the summer of 1968 in Mexico City.

In the latter part of this fourth section the authors have attempted to afford the reader further understanding of how individual athletes were dealt with by the sport psychologist accompanying them. These case studies were selected as representative of over fifty athletes who were counseled regularly prior to, and following, competition. It is hoped that careful consideration of the information in these case studies will afford greater insights into the practical realities faced by psychologists interested in the many interactions possible between the personality dynamics and performance potentials of superior athletes.

CHAPTER 11

Olympics, Mexico City, 1968

Despite several decades of psychological investigations with superior athletes, apparently only two team psychologists were present with Olympic teams in Mexico City.[1] Miroslav Vanek, the Czechoslovakian psychologist, was making his third visit to Mexico within two years with the national team. His investigations of the team's athletes had occurred over a period in excess of three years, while his personal relationships with the coaches and athletes had earned him their friendship and respect.

The team members' autobiographies had been compiled for some time and had been analyzed and studied. A number of personality tests had been administered, and the profiles obtained had provided Vanek and Hosek with additional data from which to work. These included the Cattell, Eysenck, and Mittenecker-Toman, as well as the Raven Test of Intelligence.

Data obtained from various sensory-motor tests had also been administered. Group and individual profiles had been compiled comparing individuals against norms, as well as the mean scores of various individual teams that comprised the total national team. This data had

[1] Dr. Friedrich Blanz, D.Sc., was officially assigned to the Finnish team. Dr. Blanz collected a variety of data, including personality assessments, projective tests involving drawing, and the objective feelings of athletes concerning their possible success, just prior to the time each Finnish athlete competed in Mexico City. At the time of this printing, Dr. Blanz's data has not been processed.

been collected both in Mexico City during the previous two visits of portions of the team, in 1966 and 1967, and in Prague between visits of the Czech team to Mexico. (3) Thus comparisons were also available concerning the manner in which athletes performed at home and abroad in the high altitude of Mexico City. (4) Analyses were also made concerning the responses obtained on personal interview forms at home and in the unfamiliar high altitude of the Olympic city. In summary, it was possible to make the following comparisons and cross-comparisons, using the data obtained.

1. Individual personality profiles versus norms in the personality test.

2. Mean scores on the various personality profiles of various teams, i.e., boxers, cyclists, and so on, versus norms available in the various tests.

3. Psychomotor test scores obtained in the high altitude environment of Mexico City versus the same scores obtained in Europe.

4. Psychological and psychomotor test scores obtained during the initial days, compared to the same scores obtained after residence in Mexico City for several weeks, reflecting psychological and psychomotor acclimatization. This data was available for the 1966 and 1967 visits.

5. Sociometric tests reflecting interpersonal interactions between participants of the various teams making up the national team.

6. Comparisons between personality trait scores and psychomotor test scores were available.

7. Personality trait profiles which seemed best adaptable to the high altitude, using performance data in psychomotor tests as well as performance scores in the athlete's special event, obtained in the 1966 and 1967 visits.

8. Autobiographical data could be contrasted to acclimatization (adjustment of physical performance to high altitude) and to personality trait scores.

9. Questionnaire information concerning feelings about high altitude competition could be compared to actual performance on the athlete's event, psychomotor tests, as well as scores collected on the personality profiles.

Pre-acclimatization had been also carried out in the high altitude of Austria, in the high altitude chambers in Prague, with some of the teams making up the Czech delegation during 1966 and 1967, as well as in the stressful conditions of Mexico City. During the years 1966 and 1967, various "model training" and competitive situations were arranged for various members of the Czech teams in order to study their performance under the conditions they would later meet in Mexico City. Essentially these plans transpired as follows:

In 1966 a small "model team" of twenty athletes was assembled, composed of runners at the various distances, cyclists, and one gymnast. Three coaches, two physicians, a laboratory assistant, and one psychologist accompanied the athletes. This "model team" first spent fourteen days in Prague, then went to Mexico City where they stayed for three weeks, followed by an additional fourteen days in Prague in order to study readjustment to conditions with which they were familiar.

During the initial period in Prague the athletes were tested under four conditions: in a laboratory under normal pressure, in a high-altitude chamber, in a model training session, and finally under the stress of competition. Generally the tests consisted of all-out bicycle ergometer work, which was carefully monitored, and which was immediately followed by twenty minutes of various psychomotor tests including measurements of hand-eye coordination, steadiness, tapping speed, and the like. A similar psychological battery was administered after bicycle ergometer work in the altitude chamber following interval training sessions in the field, and then all-out competition in each of the athlete's special events. Personality-trait scores were also collected in Prague during this initial fourteen days.

After moving to Mexico City in 1966 the athletes were again put through the same tests under the same conditions, with one exception. The height of Mexico City made the use of the high-altitude chamber unnecessary. Each athlete was tested every three or four days, under the conditions described, in Prague and in Mexico City. Following each day of testing, a conference was held between the physicians, the psychologist, and a coach. The first order of business that formed the basis of future discussions in this conference was the rating of each athlete in order of performance by the physician, the coach, and the psychologist, each working independently. Thus the physician rated the group of athletes tested according to physiological capacity measures he had obtained on the ergometer, the psychologist according to the psychomotor measures he had collected, while the coach rated the same athletes (from best to least capable) by observation of performance in the Olympic event in which each claimed expertise.

Following this three-week period in Mexico City, the athletes returned to Prague for one week of rest, and then spent a second week again submitting to physiological stress followed by psychomotor performance tests under the conditions previously described. Again the data was obtained in a laboratory under normal air pressure, in a high-altitude chamber under training conditions, as well as under conditions demanded by their unique event (i.e., running 800 meters).

The data collected in 1966, among other things, suggested that a more prolonged period of high-altitude training was needed before optimum performance and good psychological adjustments could be made to Mexico's high-altitude conditions. Thus in 1967 the "model team" from Czechoslovakia added another step in their training-testing regime. This time the thirty-five athletes making up the model,[2] after first being tested in Prague under the conditions described in the previous paragraphs, spent the first three weeks in Austria at an altitude comparable to that of Mexico City. They were accompanied by the same scientific team that worked with the smaller group the previous year, and again were subjected to the same testing program.

After these three weeks of altitude training in Europe in 1967 the thirty-five members again went to Mexico City. The three weeks they spent there were again accompanied by endurance tests, followed by psychomotor tests in the laboratory. There were daily meetings attended by the coach of the team evaluated that day, the physicians, and the psychologist. At the beginning of these meetings the coach would rank the team membership in order based upon the performance proficiencies he had recently observed in practice sessions. Then physicians and psychologist would both rank the players, independently, based upon the measures they had obtained from their physiological and psychological evaluations. The coach and the advising scientists would then compare these ratings, and this comparison would be used as a basis of discussion revolving around the improvement of the team's performance.

During all of the training and testing in 1966 and 1967, it was generally the practice to administer the tests to one complete team each day (the gymnasts one day, the distance runners the next, and so on). Thus the daily conference was composed of the coach of the team measured and the members of the scientific committee.

Following a three-week period in Mexico the year prior to the Olympics, the "model team" again returned to Prague. After a one-week layoff they were again tested in the laboratory under normal conditions, in the

[2] The additional athletes in this second year consisted of additional women gymnasts, a group of weightlifters, more rowers, and track-and-field athletes.

high-altitude chamber under training conditions, and under the stress of all-out performance.

At each of the testing sites additional psychological data was collected, including the Taylor Measures of Manifest Anxiety, the Moreno Sociometric Test, a personal interview form in which the following were included: athlete's attitude toward his personal performance, his feelings of subjective fatigue, his sleep habits, his appetite, his feelings of depression, elation, tensions, and similar attitudes that were likely to influence his performance. Other questions on this interview form, which was administered about every third day, included whether the athlete preferred the company of others or whether he wished to be left alone.

When the one hundred and twenty-four Czech athletes were finally selected to represent their country in 1968, a number of recommendations had been formulated.[3] The recommendations were based upon psychological, physiological, and sociometric as well as various kinds of subjective information emanating from the members of the two "model teams" constituted in 1966 and 1967.

1. Marked changes in physiological function and in coordination were found in high-altitude conditions during the initial two years. Generally, psychomotor function was found to be impaired for a period of from eight to twelve days (depending upon the athlete tested). It was recommended that a period of at least three weeks was needed to permit high-altitude acclimatization for athletes participating in events requiring high degrees of coordination.

2. The physiological data, coupled with the psychometric tests data, similarly resulted in the recommendation that athletes participating in events requiring marked cardiovascular effort be permitted at least a four-week period of acclimatization to the high altitude of Mexico City.

3. Information from the interview forms, as well as observations by coaches and by the psychologist during the "model team" testing and training carried out in 1966 and 1967, also prompted the decision that careful preparation and planning be devoted to the structuring of worthwhile and stimulating leisure-time activities for the athletes while in training and during their stay in Olympic Village. It was seen frequently that time would "hang heavy" upon athletes in training, and so a program of leisure-time recreational activities was carefully planned, taking

---

[3] The team, in addition to officials, was accompanied by three physicians, two masseurs, and one psychologist.

into consideration the preference lists submitted by the athletes on their interview forms.

These two years of investigation had also culminated in information which would be helpful to coaches. These data, containing suggestions helpful to the training of their athletes, were utilized in a training program prior to, and during, the Mexican competition. At times these suggestions aided coaches to select team members.

Some of the principles stressed in this informational program included the following:

A. It was found that the athletes should avoid overtraining, as several athletes who had passed their peaks of performance prior to arriving in Mexico during 1966 and 1967 could not regain top "form" in the high-altitude conditions. To avoid this overtraining, it was recommended that nomination of Olympic team members should occur in early June of 1968 so that athletes would experience the early "peak" in performance which would often occur shortly after being selected, and then be able to have time to attain another "peak" at the starting line in Mexico City.

B. In Mexico it was recommended that training begin slowly so that the athletes would not suffer the subjective feelings of a lowering of performance at first in the high altitude, and also avoid the fluctuations of mood frequently plotted during the 1966 and 1967 years. It was often seen, for example, that an athlete, after a few days in the high altitude, would report or evidence feelings of euphoria or elation, to be followed by a period of depression. Both these unrealistic conditions were found to be detrimental to optimum performance. Thus it was recommended to the coaches that when an athlete was brought to the high altitude he should be gradually activated and adjusted to performance in the high altitude of Mexico.[4]

C. Generally the coaches were told to help their athletes form a healthy respect for the high altitude of Mexico City. It was seen during 1966 and 1967, for example, that some athletes viewed the high altitude as a test of their manhood or courage, and attempted to brashly overcome it in a day or so. Others seemed to acquire an unhealthy fear of the altitude, particularly when their early performances were low. This latter

---

[4] The writers are aware of only three studies exploring the influence of climate and altitude upon various psychological measures of athletes. (1), (2), (5) Perhaps some of the difficult to locate research produced by military psychologists might be used in this context. The study of psychoclimatology (the influence of climate upon behavior) is in its infancy.

mental state was also detrimental to performance. Rather, it was recommended that the athletes be taught that within about twenty days their minds and bodies would mature to meet the extra stress of high altitude, and that they should not overreact one way or the other prior to that time, but should faithfully train under the direction of their coach.

D. The data further suggested that training of athletes in high altitudes prior to competition is of help in achieving superior performance independent of whether the competition occurs in high altitude or at sea level. For example, in 1967 it was found that following three weeks in Austria and then three weeks in Mexico City, some of the best lifetime performances were achieved by the athletes tested *after their return to Prague* (elevation about one thousand feet above sea level)!

Thus it was suggested that high-altitude training in endurance events be engaged in in addition to progressive resistance exercises, interval training, and similar innovations that have been incorporated into athlete training regimes during the past several decades. The observation that runners from high altitudes seemed to do extremely well in long-distance races was, therefore, confirmed by scientific laboratory tests.

E. The coaches were further cautioned to prepare their athletes intellectually for the conditions at Mexico City. In this way fluctuations in an athlete's mood, performances, and level of activation might be avoided.

The Czech team arrived at Mexico City early. Many of the team members had been investigated during the 1966 and 1967 "model" training programs. The physicians and psychologists were personally acquainted with each athlete. Their coaches had been participating in a pre-Olympic training program in Prague. All one hundred twenty-four members had been tested in the batteries of tests described in the preceding pages following their nomination to the team in 1968, by teams of physicians and psychologists.[5]

The psychologists had surmised, as a result of previous investigations, that about 15 to 20 per cent of all superior performers are what might be termed problem athletes. This was also true of the Czech Olympic team. Thus the team psychologist was prepared to focus much of his attention upon this subgroup and to work with them in psychotherapeutic ways.

The observations of the physicians and coaches, together with those

[5] In addition to Miroslav Vanek, the team of psychologists included Drs. Vaclav Hosek, Franticek Mann, and Peter Knotek.

of the psychologists, revealed that in addition to these problem athletes, there were a larger number of athletes who seemed at times to experience minor psychological difficulties in connection with their performance.

In addition, athletes themselves came to the psychologist with problems that they felt he might help them to overcome. Over-all, about one half of the team fell into one of these groups (that is, problem athletes or athletes with minor difficulties identified either by the coach or through self-referral).

During the initial days in Olympic Village the psychologist aided in dealing with newspapermen, acting as an interpreter, setting up facilities, and in formulating a recreational schedule. However, as time wore on, more and more of his time was taken up with formal and informal interviews with athletes composing the team. Each day one or two teams were observed in training and, when thought advisable, informal conversations were instituted by the psychologist. These would frequently start by dwelling on general subjects, but many times would terminate in the identification of a problem of some type.

If there seemed little time to deal with the difficulty unveiled at the training area or in the dining room, special time was scheduled for the purpose of a private interview in the psychologist's room. At other times a brief word at the practice site seemed to suffice.

During the six weeks the team was on the Olympic site (four weeks pre-training, two weeks competition), a total of over two hundred formal interviews were scheduled in which the problems of about fifty-five athletes were discussed. In addition to these interviews, numerous informal discussions were held with athletes on their training sites or in the dining or living areas. Prior to each interview scheduled the athlete's personal file containing the results of his personality and psychomotor test data would be consulted. These would be reviewed again if the interviewed person revealed some unexpected problems.

The number of interviews with women was proportional to the number on the team. About one third of the team membership were women.

In addition to individual interviews, the psychologist conducted (at the invitation of the coaches) group discussions, with various sports teams making up the national contingent. On these occasions behavior with other national teams, behavior within the group, as well as individual problems were discussed. Of particular interest to the athletes in these group discussions were the performance oscillations they often experienced just prior to competition. Motivation was a frequent topic during these meetings and attempts were made to advance reasons why a group of athletes or an individual athlete should "try harder" or why an individual might attempt to motivate himself to greater effort. During these group interviews, athletes were urged to ask questions of the psychologist and these were answered to the best of his ability.

The kinds of problems that emerged during the individual interviews were of several types. Some of the problems revolved around the athlete's private life, for example, the absence of letters from home, or sick children, often caused the athlete some anxiety. Marital problems plagued other athletes.

A second classification of problems revolved around inter-group relationships in the group with which the athlete was housed. The athlete's relationships with teammates as well as with his coaches often caused him to worry. There were occasional reports of feelings of hostility directed toward him by teammates and/or other officials.

A third type of problem centered upon the athlete's performance in the competition. As competition approached, the importance of slight injuries or sicknesses was often magnified in the athlete's mind.

A fourth type of problem that concerned athletes was their future after competition. Some were worried about their professional futures. Their choice of occupation as it related to, or was independent from, athletics caused some athletes to seek the counsel of the psychologist. Others sought help concerning whether they should remain in competition after the Olympics.

Some of the problems could be solved by direct and obvious action. For example, a lack of communication at home could be remedied by a phone call. If letters from the family were not forthcoming, the family was often contacted and reminded that their relative sought some communication from them.

To prevent homesickness, Czech art objects and pictures were brought in to the village and placed in the rooms. Records and tapes of Czech music were also provided, as was beer brewed in Pilsen, Czechoslovakia.

To relieve boredom and excess tension connected with competition, special trips and excursions had been arranged. These included trips to movies and to historical points around Mexico City.[6]

[6] Data collected prior to coming to Mexico concerning preferences of athletes for various leisure-time activities suggested that they valued highly the opportunity to take sightseeing trips. However, shortly after arriving, the same questionnaire revealed a distinct shift in preferences. After several days in Olympic Village the athletes indicated a preference for more relaxed leisure-time activities, such as listening to music, and the like, as more and more the impending competition seemed to occupy their thoughts.

Similarly, problems centered around injury could be solved upon consultation with a physician. Positive prognosis from a physician concerning an athlete's momentary feelings of discomfort often helped the athlete toward a more positive viewpoint.

The use of psychodrama or interviews with coaches could often solve problems centering around inter-personal relationships in Olympic Village. Some athletes needed solitude, and their living quarters were arranged to permit this when it seemed to be called for. At times inter-personal problems were remediated, with group conferences among roommates concerning the use of a radio, being quiet during sleeping hours, and similar problems. Athletes were counseled concerning their teammate's needs for friendship and association when this seemed called for.

Other problems could not be solved so simply. In general, however, the athlete with a more serious problem could be given some kind of perspective that could enable him to handle it in the future. At times the problem was eased somewhat simply because the athlete was permitted to talk about it to someone. This latter kind of problem generally hinged around some personal relationships between the athlete and his wife or girl friend.

Of the fifty-five athletes who were formally interviewed, about fifteen were only seen once by the psychologist. The remainder visited the psychologist between four and six times. Many of the athletes preferred to talk at great length, and some of the interviews lasted throughout the night. This type of prolonged interview would frequently be held after competition, as many of the athletes had difficulty calming themselves down following the high level of activation to which they had raised themselves. Other interviews lasted only twenty minutes.

If the athlete was overaroused, Schultz Autogenne training was often employed during many of the interviews. After competition, if activation remained too high, relaxants were administered to induce sleep.

The psychologist tried to meet each athlete on the team following competition if for nothing more than to extend congratulations. It was especially deemed important to interview the losers more than once following competition. During these interviews it was often attempted to reduce excess intra- and extra-punitive aggression as a result of the frustration of losing. The athlete was encouraged to examine himself and to find constructive methods for improving his own performance, rather than to blame others, or in a destructive way to blame himself for his failure or his success in competition. In many cases this type of interview was repeated three or four times.

The athlete was given the opportunity to think about his past performance during the time between interviews. The athlete was not told why, during these interviews, but was encouraged to find the answers himself for his lack of success. The psychologist frequently professed ignorance of the intricacies of the athlete's sport, but instead attempted to pose questions to which the athlete would often seek his own answers. About 70 per cent of the losing athletes interviewed in this way would indeed seem to arrive, with therapeutic benefits, at the logical answers for their lack of sucess. Frequently the athlete needed a listener after he had lost. Thus the psychologist did not attempt to overdirect the interview, nor to dominate the conversation.

The successful athletes who had been previously interviewed, on the other hand, evidenced three primary kinds of reactions to the psychologist following competition. On the part of about 50 per cent of these athletes the reaction was neutral. This kind of bland reaction seemed almost like some kind of defensive mechanism, with the athlete not quite knowing whether to thank or to ignore the psychologist.[7] There seemed to be a reluctance on the part of these athletes to permit anyone else to participate in their success. This reaction is understandable, as the competitive situation abounds with those who would share in the athlete's hard-won success. However, it was felt by the psychologist that if he had attempted, even to the slightest degree, to claim some credit for the athlete's success, all rapport in the future between him and any other athletes would diminish. Athletes are sensitive to a "grab for glory" by "parasites" within the athletic environment. If the psychologist proves to be one of these, it seems certain that his future effectiveness may be minimal.

Another reaction of successful performers toward the psychologist following competition took the form of cool hostility. Similar to the individual taking a neutral stance, this athlete also seemed to be protecting his glory from one who might attempt to claim part of the credit for it. His behavior seemed to say, "While you may have helped me prior to competition, my success is my own, and you may in no way share it. Furthermore, our relationship is at an end."

[7] Successful athletes are defined not only as those who won medals, but also those whose performances exceeded their previous best, and/or those who performed better than expected in the competition.

The third type of post-competitive façade toward the psychologist was a friendly one. This was manifested in several ways. For example, effusive thanks were often extended, others suggested that part of the medal won belonged to their counselor.

Care was taken by the psychologist not to evidence any kind of emotional response to any of these reactions by the successful athletes. If he were to return the hostility shown him, for example, it is likely that the team members would not come to him in the future if they should need help. If he was not impersonal to the grateful participant, others would observe the "sharing of the glory" and might become alienated. If the psychologist was not amiable to the cool and neutral approach, again he was likely to elicit hostility from others who might view it as an attempt to share in the limelight of success.

In the post-Olympic conference attended by coaches, physicians, and other team officials, the worth of all those connected with the Czech team was evaluated. The evaluation accorded the team psychologist was a positive one. It was believed that the sport psychologist was useful to the team, and it appeared that as far as the Czech Olympic team was concerned, the position of the sport psychologist was a secure one in future competitions.

Furthermore, it seemed that the coaches viewed the intervention of the psychologist in helpful ways. It appears that future work of the psychologist on teams engaged in high-level competition will be successful to the extent to which helpful communication is achieved between the team coach, the physician, and the psychologist. The physician and the psychologist can be most helpful if they remain fixed to their respective areas of expertise and work through the coach when attempting to upgrade athletic performance. Presuming to be experts in the tactics and qualifications for a particular sport is likely to alienate the coach to this kind of ancillary assistance.

Essentially, therefore, it appears that to achieve the most success, the sport psychologist should affix his attention upon the component of the athlete's personality and of team interactions that his background qualifies him to evaluate, and leave other matters to the team coach. Any communication between an athlete and the psychologist should be transmitted to the coach, so that the latter will not feel bypassed in any way. Finally, it is imperative that the psychologist on teams be content to assume a service role and that he be discreet in his professional dealings, rather than placing himself in positions in which he appears to be sharing in the glory of individual and/or team successes.

REFERENCES

1. Azatan, M. "K Izuceniju Funkcii Centralnoj Nervnoj Sistemy u Sportsmenov u Periode Aklimatizacii" (The Central Nervous System of Sportsmen and the Period of Acclimatization). Mat. IX Uses. Nac. Konf. (*Proceedings* of the Ninth All-Union Scientific Conference), Kaunas, 1966.
2. Canchasvili, S., and Bakuradze, G. "Izmenije Ostroty Ipolja Zrenija u Sportsmenov pod Vlijanim Trenirovki v Uslovijach Srednegora" (The Influence of Training in the Middle Altitude upon Visual Functions), Mat. IX Uses. Nac. Konf. (*Proceedings* of the Ninth All-Union Scientific Conference), Kaunas, 1966.
3. Horak, J., and Komadel, L. "Slozeni a Ukoly Csl. Vypravy pri II Predolympijskem Tydnu a Zdravotni Stau Behem Pobytu v Mexicu" (The Team and the Aims of the Czechoslovakian Expedition in the Second Pre-Olympic Week and the State of Health During the Time in Mexico). *Teorie a Praxe Telesne Vychovy*, Prague, **16**:7, 1968.
4. Schonholzer, G. *Sport in Mittlerer Höhe* (Sport Activity in the Middle Altitude). Bern: Haupt, Paul, 1967.
5. Tune, G. S. "Psychological Effects of Hypoxis: Review of Certain Literature from the Period 1950 to 1963." *Perceptual and Motor Skills*, **19**:2, 1964.

CHAPTER 12

Case Studies

Despite the collections of norms and the information collected from group surveys of sociometric evaluations, the primary concern of the sport psychologist is the individual athlete and his drives, motives, and performances. It is his job to elicit optimum performances from athletes, whether they be exhibiting their prowess individually or as an important team member.

Athletes, like nonathletes, are highly individual in nature. They come in many sizes and with many kinds of personality traits and psychomotor abilities. Some athletes are sociable and outgoing, just as are some nonathletes, while others are introverted and withdrawn.

There are, however, several distinguishable athlete types. There are consistent kinds of individuals participating in athletics who to some degree exhibit similar personalities, reactions to stresses, and failures and successes in athletic participation.

The case histories that follow represent world-class athletes with whom the co-author has dealt in his job as psychologist for the Czechoslovakian Olympic team. The authors have attempted to alter the narratives so that the individuals discussed will not be recognized.

The "athletic types" discussed in the following case histories are not necessarily "problem athletes," but simply represent some of the individuals who will be encountered on a team. Beisser (1) and Ogilvie

167

and Tutko (2) have devoted entire texts to delineating the personality dynamics of individual athletes.

The following narratives are more an attempt to classify and discuss various categories of athletes' problems than an effort to outline specific ways of remediating "special hang-ups" sometimes seen in superior athletes and in other individuals attempting to exhibit high-level performances in a number of stressful occupations and avocations.

These discussions are organized in the following manner. Initially, the performance characteristics of the athlete are presented. Second, the motivations of the individuals are covered. Third, the psychological characteristics of the athletes evaluated with various personality scales are discussed. Fourth, the types of problems facing the athletes are explored. Each section concludes with a description of the ways in which the team psychologist interacted with the athlete and the strategies he used to aid him (or her) to overcome problems encountered.

Five case studies are presented. The first deals with an athlete who characteristically exhibited better performance in practice than he did in competition—a problem not uncommon in athletes. The second tells about an athlete whose motivations were difficult to assess, and describes how a psychologist evaluated his motivational structure incorrectly. The third reveals how a superior athlete exhibited positive psychological traits that somehow permitted him to raise himself to optimum performance during competition—performance that was usually superior to his efforts during practice. The fourth describes how a self-sufficient athlete, after an extensive evaluation, courteously rejected the help of the psychologist just prior to the most important competition of her career. The fifth discusses the manner in which an athlete's neurotic fixation upon the inability to perform well in a recreational activity interacted with his success in another sport in which he evidenced a high level of proficiency.

The studies reviewed represent only five out of many that could be described by the authors. It is felt, however, that the ones selected are not only representative but are also among the most interesting with which the authors are familiar.

REFERENCES

1. Beisser, Arnold H. *The Madness in Sports.* New York: Appleton-Century-Crofts, 1967.
2. Ogilvie, B., and Tutko, T. *Problem Athletes and How to Handle Them.* New York: Ronald Press, 1966.

Case Study 1

Performance Characteristics

Jan, a field event performer, was concerned as he approached world competition. He worried about what others would learn of his performance in practice and in warm-up meets. He voiced the desire to perform poorly so that others in the world would not know his true ability and thus he could establish himself as a favorite in the coming Olympics.

Adding to Jan's worries was the fact that his world record in his event was bettered just prior to the Olympics by a foreign competitor—a world record that he held for three years. He thus claimed that if he excelled in practice and became one of the favorites, his chances to succeed in Olympic competition would be influenced negatively.

Jan's practice throws fluctuated from day to day and from competition to competition during the two years prior to the Olympics. In the previous Olympics he had posted the best marks prior to competition, but he had failed to win the gold medal in his event. It was perhaps due to this previous failure as a favorite that he seemed reluctant to assume the same role in the coming contest of skill and strength among world-class athletes.

Thus as the second Olympics approached, Jan's competitive marks failed to reach those marks posted in training and, at the same time, his performance in competition deteriorated. He became increasingly more irritable and refused to work with a coach. He seemed jealous of his competitors whether they were from his own country or from other parts of the world. His manner reflected the attitude of "Who can help

me to better myself when I am already the best in the world?" And he
ignored his friends, who attempted to convince him to accept help from
knowledgeable tutors.

Jan thus trained himself. He would tell all who listened that he was
training hard, when actually he was not doing so. He showed a lack
of self-control that prevented him from extending himself in practice.
His self-preparations interfered with invitations to contests abroad,
contests that would have helped him to better himself.

Throughout this period his objective performance was not equal to
his self-descriptions of his prowess. He appeared to be attempting to
create an impression of omnipotence, while his actual ability continued
to deteriorate. He performed badly in some of the second-level competitions carried out in his own country; hence his countrymen lost
faith in his abilities and many of them doubted that he would win an
Olympic medal.

Motivation

Jan's achievement needs were high. In competitions in which he and
the other competitors would meet such adverse conditions as rain and
wind, he would vaunt that he was best equipped to overcome problems
encountered in meets, and hence that he stood the best chance to win.

An important secondary motive that influenced Jan's performance
was an economic one. He realized that only with continued success in
his event could he hope to maintain the relatively high standard of living to which he had become accustomed and that he had come to enjoy.
He had prepared himself in no profession other than in performing well
in his Olympic event. He was well aware of the economic and social
consequences of failure, and he knew that if he were to fail, he would
face hard times after his competitive days.

While Jan voiced his desire to obtain a gold medal, it was also true
that either a second, a third, a fourth, or even a fifth place in the Olympic
competition would meet his psychological and material needs. He would
say at times that he would be satisfied to be numbered among the first
five in the world, while at other times he stated that perhaps he could
win in an upset. He thus seemed to be attempting to absolve himself
of the responsibility of winning—responsibility that he had not borne well
previously. In the previous Olympic competition he and the other athletes
who knew his record were surprised when he *did not* win, while in the

coming Olympics surprise would be registered if he *did* win. In the previous Olympics his role was that of a pressure-ridden and exposed favorite. In the forthcoming competition he began to assume the less-threatened role of one of the top six favorites.

Personality Traits

Personality tests administered to Jan revealed that high needs for achievement were accompanied by several traits that were likely to interfere with his performance. He evidenced a high need for the assumption of a kind of "halo" effect. He proved to be introverted, and at times he would exhibit paranoid tendencies. His level of sociability was low and frequently his behavior to most of his associates would be hostile.

He could not take a joke played on him, although he was not reluctant to play jokes on others. One evening, for example, he laughed when he observed another athlete slightly wetting the sheets of his team members. However, on another evening when this type of joke was played on him, he became so angry that he wanted to fight everyone in the room.

Jan tended to try to dominate those around him. His frustration tolerance was low and he would evidence extrapunitive reactions to frustrations for a bad performance—reactions such as blaming other people and conditions rather than blaming himself. When he lost, he would invariably blame either the judges, the equipment, the climate, or an old injury. If he were told that his loss was his own fault, he would withdraw and leave his accuser. He became suspicious of all efforts to help him to improve.

Jan's I.Q. was average. At times he would seem to be aware that others on the team were intellectually superior, but he would be careful not to show his awareness of their superiority. He was once observing two other athletes taking part in a test of ingenuity that was devised by the psychologist in order to pass leisure time. He ridiculed one of the athletes who seemed to be less adroit, but he was quick to turn down the challenge offered to him by the other athletes to solve the problem posed by the test. He also liked to demonstrate his purported language ability and seldom passed up opportunities to use foreign terms. However, the terms that he chose would often be incorrect and inappropriate to the situation.

Jan's tension level was high. His moods fluctuated from one day to the next and were characterized by feelings of depression alternating with feelings of elation. He also resisted attempts by the scientists to investigate his physiological and psychological characteristics. He appeared to have high need for status and dignity; he wanted to be respected. He proved to be sensitive to even the slightest social rebuff, imagining that he had been slighted when in truth this was not so.

If he were given criticism about his performance in front of other team members, he would characteristically vent his anger in a few choice phrases, stomp from the practice area and refuse to work any more that day. He viewed the coach only as an instrument to enhance his glory and not as an individual who should find fault with him or with his performance. He was careful to hide his fear of failure from his fellow athletes.

Jan's outward behavior attempted to project confidence—confidence that in truth he did not feel. He seemed to feel particularly inferior about his educational status. He would frequently make derogatory remarks about college-educated teammates and about the scientists who accompanied the team. He appeared to be of the opinion that if everyone were able to perform physically as well as he could, there would be no need to go to colleges and universities.

Psychological Preparation

The initial attempt on the part of the psychologist was to win Jan's confidence. Frequent discussions were held during which the psychologist reinforced the athlete's feelings of dominance by assuming a subordinate role. The problems that were discussed were often those of the psychologist, so that the athlete would neither feel that he was being talked down to nor that he was somehow losing his superior role.

During these informal discussions the psychologist attempted to ascertain what motivated Jan; whether it was the prestige of winning, the respect of his family, the respect of his countrymen, or dominance over his competitors. Others were also consulted about the motives that may have been paramount to Jan. Discussions were held with his previous coaches, his fellow athletes, and those with whom he had come in contact during the years.

The first contacts between Jan and the psychologist took place at infrequent intervals and continued over a period of approximately one year. Following this initial period of time, the psychologist had ascertained that he had gained the athlete's confidence. He then invited Jan to a formal interview.

During this talk the psychologist explained to Jan that he realized his problem, the stress of competition facing him, and he offered his help in meeting the coming contest. He further explained that scores from a group of psychological tests would be helpful to him, and he requested permission to administer the tests. The athlete was also assured that all that transpired between them would be held in complete confidence and that he should not tell others about his collaboration with the psychologist.

At the termination of this interview the athlete indicated his desire to cooperate, and a battery of tests was administered. During this initial investigation the athlete would frequently evidence hostility and at other times indifference. The psychologist was careful to explain that it did not matter to him whether Jan lost or won, but that he was interesting as an individual case independent of his athletic attainment.

When Jan was shown the results of the investigations, he became fascinated with the findings and began to evidence trust in the behavioral scientist, who had apparently won his respect and friendship. At this point the roles played by the athlete and the psychologist underwent a change. The initial submissive role assumed by the psychologist was discarded as the athlete was informed in a frank and at times brutal way about the personality deficiencies uncovered in the examination.

Jan, on the other hand, became submissive. The psychologist was careful at this point to never evidence this kind of role reversal in the presence of other people, and would enhance the superior and dominating role of the athlete whenever it was convenient to do so. When others would speak about the athlete in derogatory terms, the psychologist would defend him, particularly when taunts were leveled against him about his coming competition. With continued interaction of this type, the athlete began to trust the psychologist to an increased degree.

When the athlete and the psychologist reached Olympic Village, it was obvious to both that Jan's depressions were lower and, as competition was approaching, his periods of elation were higher. Then after a week Jan approached the psychologist for help. His tensions were becoming almost unbearable; so the psychologist, with the aid of a physician, administered a mild sedative to help him to sleep soundly at night.

Then during a period of deep depression Jan again sought out the psychologist. This time he was given a stimulant. Following these pharmaceutical administrations, the athlete began to feel that his high periods of tension were under reasonable control and that his depressions were similarly not as marked. During this period the athlete's confidence in the psychologist seemed strengthened and confirmed.

At this point the psychologist suggested to Jan that relaxation training administered independent of any kind of sedatives or stimulants could be even more helpful. Thus the psychologist administered relaxation training every second day following practice and before sleep. The timing of these training periods coincided with the athlete's schedules and needs. The training followed the Schultz method previously described.

Ten days prior to Olympic competition, the relaxation training was administered and was followed by techniques that attempted to activate the athlete to levels high enough to deal with the demands of the coming contest. This same relaxation training was carried out the night prior to Jan's efforts in the final Olympic competition, while the next day, two hours before competition, relaxation training was followed by techniques that purported to induce activation.

In competition Jan was successful and posted his best effort of the year. His mark left him in the top five in his event, and was better than he had earned in either of the two Olympic competitions in which he had participated. What seemed most significant, however, was the fact that Jan, after watching the actual winner's superior efforts, continued to improve rather than to "wilt," as his fellow competitors seemed to do upon viewing these same efforts. His mark also exceeded the best he had been able to exhibit during his pre-Olympic training.

After competition Jan returned in some ways to his previous mode of behavior toward the psychologist. His rather neutral attitude upon winning indicated that he was testing the psychologist, observing his actions to determine whether or not he could continue to trust him. His manner seemed to reflect that if the psychologist were not trying to share in his glory of winning, then he would continue their collaboration.

Summary

In dealing with Jan, the initial phase consisted of three stages. The first included the making of frequent and informal attempts to assess the athlete. The second was to win his confidence and to permit him to maintain his dominant role. The third stage was to cause a role reversal to occur so that respect could be gained and a formal assessment of his personality could be gotten. And it was important here that the psychologist did not reveal to others the nature of this reversal of status positions.

The intermediate phase followed as the period of time during which Jan was confronted with the results of the personality assessment and was given positive help; first by way of stimulants and sedatives, and second by way of relaxation training.

The final phase transpired following competition. During this period the roles again semeed to reverse themselves. Now the athlete realized his goals and reinforced his needs for achievement, dominance, and success, while the psychologist was also content with the part his ministrations had played and at the same time declined to "steal the limelight" from Jan.

The psychological testing was an important source of basic information, but in this case it was used as a "weapon" through which the psychologist could control the dominating athlete. More important than the test scores, however, was the sensitivity of the psychologist to the athlete's emotional states and mood changes during the informal and the formal interviews.

Case Study 2

Performance Characteristics

Robert was thirty years old, and had engaged in a combative sport for his country for the past ten years. His performances during this time ranged the success scale. He won at Rome, did poorly at Tokyo, and again won the European championships in his sport just prior to the Olympics in Mexico City.

He trained hard, but generally ignored his coaches. He prepared himself physically to a high degree and at the same time had gained experience. He was not overly aggressive and usually did not win his matches immediately, but by decisions.

As the Mexican Olympics were upon him, he felt his prowess waning to some degree. Although he had trained hard, he felt that some of his speed and strength were leaving him and he hoped to compensate for the loss of these by relying upon his experience in international competitions. Robert was aware, as were those who watched him, that his athletic career was nearing its end.

The results of physiological evaluations of his condition confirmed what was observed—that he was in good shape. He was ready to try again and to rely, as he had in the past, upon his guile rather than upon bullish strength. In general, he was observed to be overestimating his ability just prior to his final major contest.

Since his recent win in the European championships, his teammates and countrymen expected a gold medal from him in Mexico. He too greatly coveted another win in international competition. Another triumph would give him status above and beyond continued social and economic status in his country, the normal one given to his job. His regular career was that of a soldier, a position in society not comparable to that of an athlete revered by the public.

Motivation

The team psychologist, after many conversations with Robert, reasoned that his primary motives included high needs for achievement and glory for his family. He stated, for example, that he had promised his third child a medal from his trip to Mexico City. He kept pictures of his family on the walls of his living quarters and close by when competing. He even had asked spectators to call out "for your family . . . for your wife" and similar exhortations while he was competing to spur him to greater heights.

It was also apparent that Robert's performance resulted from secondary material motives. He had planned to buy a new car when returning to his country after the Olympics. He also believed that he would achieve officer status in the army upon winning in Mexico City, and at the same time had begun to make arrangements to have his home remodeled while he was in Mexico. Few of these economic and social improvements could be carried out if he failed to do well in his final competition. None of them were possible as a common soldier in the army.

His materialistic tendencies were further evidenced in the "sharp trading" he carried on in Olympic Village with athletes from other countries. He seemed to end up with more and better trinkets from the other athletes when this trading was completed each day, and would brag about his successful transactions. Robert seemed to be able to begin each day with nothing and to end up with an armful of barter. His ability as a "horse trader" grew. Some who did not have the time nor the guile to make clever exchanges came to him and, for a profit, he turned their goods into more expensive and more interesting souvenirs.

Personality Characteristics

His general demeanor was a bragging one. Robert felt superior to his fellow athletes, and did not decline to show it. He was extroverted, selfish, and generally unsociable even though he was outgoing with people in a superficial way. He seemed to be measuring everyone he met according to what he could gain from them for himself and for his family.

Robert's behavior was usually domineering to his fellow team members and to those around him. But when team officials were in close proximity, he often assumed a submissive attitude. He seemed to be constantly "playing politics," attempting to please his superiors while "working" his equals for his own personal, athletic, and material gains.

On several occasions he would approach team officials with a joke, attempting to curry their favor with a clownlike attitude. But he was trying too hard to please, and his teammates were openly hostile to him as a result.

His ambiguous behavior and feelings were often vocalized; he imagined that his teammates all hated him, but that he loved them all in spite of this. He assumed the role of a frank, goodhearted boy who was at times misunderstood by those around him but who, underneath it all, was pious and good to others. In reality he was sly, astute, and mildly dishonest in his dealings with others.

One characteristic incident is that of a coach who was going to take a trip to a nearby town. Robert knew that the coach's room would be unoccupied during his absence. So he set about badgering the physicians, the coaches, and the team psychologist with tales of his growing insomnia. He complained that his roommates with their noise kept him awake and that he had to run to exhaustion to become tired enough to be able to sleep. As a result he obtained the coach's private room when the coach vacated it. Robert's feelings of self-importance were further enhanced by his apparently successful performance carried out in the presence of those who could give him what he wanted. The officials, the physicians, and the coaches, on the other hand, realized that his complaints were probably an act, but they felt that they had to humor him and to let him have his way because of his potential success in the coming competition.

Robert's high needs for dominance were evidenced in a number of ways. He constantly tried to get more for himself in most situations, and he usually took an indirect route rather than a direct one to accomplish this. At one point he attempted to acquire a new pair of shoes by claiming that his old shoes, bought in his native country, did not fit. But he was not dissuaded when the head of his country's delegation turned him down. Instead he started to brag about his newly acquired room, and he criticized his teammates as stupid for not having attempted the same strategy to obtain better quarters. If he had acquired the new shoes in the same manner, those shoes also would have been used to assert the superiority over his teammates.

Robert's frustration tolerance and his emotional stability were low. His I.Q. was slightly below average despite the guile that he frequently evidenced in practical matters. In both the Eysenck and the Cattell tests the scores obtained reflected the tendency of his moods to change frequently and unexpectedly. Scores obtained from Taylor's Scale of Manifest Anxiety reflected a high level of anxiety. Scores on personality tests suggested that he was patient.

One example of Robert's patience was the evening that he lost a game of checkers to a bright teammate. He insisted that the games continue until he had won. But as his opponent was considerably more intelligent, the games continued until early the following morning; and it became evident that only by his adversary permitting him to win would the marathon be allowed to terminate.

Robert's patience was also evidenced in the trading business that he carried out around Olympic Village. He would wait many days in order to gain an advantage in some kind of trade; that is, to acquire an article that he coveted and that he believed had value.

But despite Robert's apparent psychological instability, his physiological stability was high. His respiration, his blood pressure, and the like, did not evidence any marked or frequent changes when he was exposed to stressful conditions, when he was preparing himself to meet a threat of some kind, or when he was competing.

Robert was conservative and was not very creative in his thought processes. He generally declined to take a risk and, when meeting his opponents, he only committed himself when he was sure of an advantage. In competition, he was neither a reckless trader nor an adversary. These qualities were reflected in his personal life as well as in his competitive career.

Psychological Preparation

Robert's attitude toward the scientists evaluating him was generally a negative one. But since he assumed that they were important personages within the Olympic team, he was verbally respectful to them when they were within earshot. Although he had no idea what a psychologist was or how one functioned, he tried to gain the friendship and interest of the one who was accompanying the team. And in order to curry favor he would feign problems in the middle of the night, complaining that he was worried and that he could not sleep. Then he would concoct reasons for his worries that needed discussion, in order to attempt to make the psychologist feel important and needed.

During the initial days in Olympic Village the psychologist, on the other hand, decided to pursue a direct and open approach with the athlete. A formal interview was requested; and when Robert arrived, he was presented with the data that had been collected on him, including his test profiles and test scores.

The psychologist explained to Robert that he was aware of the several "games" that he was playing in Olympic Village. He was told that he would be neither helped in carrying out some of his materialistic efforts in trading nor helped in obtaining that pair of shoes. He was told that it was obvious that the forthcoming competition was one of his last contests, and that it meant a great deal in terms of a future coaching career and of future social and economic status. The psychologist offered to help him to win, or at least to do his best, but said, on the other hand, he would not be given help in obtaining some of the petty comforts and trinkets which he seemed intent upon acquiring.

Robert, being both sensitive and tense, seemed to understand and to be willing to cooperate. He appeared to accept the role of the psychologist and to understand the potential help that was being offered. He remarked to the psychologist that he seemed to know him better than his wife did. The psychologist worked with him in an informal manner during the days prior to competition, and as many as fifteen meetings were held.

Special pains were taken to attempt to uncover Robert's motives for competing. Robert continually emphasized that his family was the paramount motivating force in his life. He frequently spoke of his children and of the devotion that his wife had for him. He would show the psychologist the shopping that he had done for his family by displaying the items that he was able to acquire for each member.

Robert presented a believable story. It indeed indicated that the primary motivating force in his life was his family. When he shopped, his purchases were never for himself, but always for some member of his family. The psychologist was read letters from Robert's home—letters that described how his wife was exhorting him to train hard and to win his contests.

During these interviews Robert also admitted his fear of competing, particularly competing in the first match. But following his initial encounter, he explained, his fears would lessen, and the remaining ones were usually less stressful to him.

Because Robert evidenced inordinately high-tension levels, he was subjected to various relaxation techniques, particularly those outlined by Schultz. These sessions were carried out in a period of ten nights. Prior to this help Robert had habitually attempted to run off his tensions at night but, after being exposed to these methods, he sought a more passive means of alleviating his excess anxiety and tensions. He viewed these late-night relaxation sessions as a special privilege, and his participation in them seemed to enhance his feelings of dominance. The psychologist was aware of this but carried them out anyway because they seemed helpful. After such sessions Robert reported that he slept more soundly.

Three days before competition Robert evidenced a high level of self-confidence. He spoke about the "next" competition, as if the impending competition was completed and he had been successful in it. His first adversary in the Olympic competition was unknown to him, and he knew only that he was a man considerably younger than he was. In reality his first opponent was not only younger, but stronger and tougher, although lacking in some of the experience and technique possessed by the older athlete.

During the evening before competition Robert appeared relaxed, and got a good night's sleep. But upon leaving for the arena two hours before the match, his tension was high; he evidenced a pulse rate of 125 beats per minute, voiced a desire to "kill" his opponent, said he "was ready for anything," and continually jumped around. His physical movement, in fact, was generally excessive.

Robert usually required a special seat on the bus when traveling with his teammates. However, on this occasion he sought the company of the psychologist. He complained of his high tension and asked if he could be relaxed. During the trip the team psychologist administered relaxation training with Robert lying across three seats. After ten minutes of this type of training the psychologist attempted to activate him to a high level, suggesting that he would be fighting for his family, since this seemed to be the primary motivating force in his life. This suggested activation was repeated for five minutes at the end of the bus ride.

In the dressing room before competition Robert appeared very quiet. The match itself was a catastrophe. The fighter he was facing was indeed younger and tougher, and he was defeated soundly.

Following this first and final match, Robert informed the psychologist that his loss was caused by his pre-start tranquillity. He further offered that in his previous successful starts he needed to elicit in himself enormous fear by dwelling upon the possibility of physical fear and physical deformation of his face. He was able to engender this fear, he added, because with physical injury would purportedly come a loss of the ability to support his family, as well as the loss of the love of his wife.

The psychologist concluded, after reflecting upon the events before, during, and after the match, that the pre-competition psychological preparation had not been well thought out. The primary mistake, it was concluded, was in the fact that the activation period was accomplished by reference to events and motives only indirectly connected with the fight—those connected with his family. Rather the athlete should have been activated by suggestions that the fight itself would be hard and tough, that his opponent was to be a formidable adversary, and that the contest could easily result in injury, defeat, or, if he struggled hard enough, in glory and victory.

Case Study 3

Performance Characteristics

The archer's performance was consistent and good. Dick was near world-record form and his physical condition was excellent. In every competition he entered, his score was near his best, or nearly so.

Observers of his performance were suspicious because of the excellent scores he would post and suggested, at times, that it was because he seemed to habitually use relaxants prior to shooting. His use of these relaxants, however, was not an unusual practice for individuals competing in this sport, and the kind and amount he took were not contrary to international agreements. The doping laws some felt he might be violating, in truth, are not very exact and deal primarily with the use of stimulants, not relaxants.

Motivation

One of the primary joys in his life was his archery, and this was accompanied by a high need for achievement in this skill. He had practiced about ten years, shooting every day from three to four hours. He and his teammates attempted to enhance their general physical condition in other ways, such as by running, by lifting weights, and by engaging in high jumping and broad jumping.

His economic motives were not attached to his athletic prowess. He had an excellent job. He had graduated from the university with a major in architecture and worked in a responsible position in one of the leading construction companies in his city. He was not likely to attract national recognition nor gain financial advantages from his sports participation, and he knew it. He had a comfortable home, a car, and a secure family life. Thus his dedication to archery was for its own sake, not for any kind of possible auxiliary rewards which might accompany his successful performance in it.

Dick's family shared his interest in his sport and would train with him and at times enter competitions themselves. It was described as an "archery family." His aim in future competition was to post a world record and probably he strove to do this in order to achieve increased status in his family and particularly in the eyes of his boys. He would often say to his boys, for example, that "hard training and self-discipline is the only way to bring rewards." He then would demonstrate how hard he could train by not only working hard but also abstaining from smoking and drinking. He also claimed that after achieving a world record, he would terminate his sports career, although his age (he was 32) did not necessarily warrant this.

Personality Traits

Dick's test scores and general demeanor revealed him to be introverted and reserved. He was emotionally unstable in some ways, particularly when tension and pressure on his performance would mount. He remained relaxed and calm, however, when engaged in his work outside the sports domain. Characteristic of this type of event is the increase of pressure on the performer as successful and successive rounds are shot. To obtain perfect or near-perfect scores becomes more difficult as competition wears on. And frequently during his last series of shots, because he knew he might reach a world's record, his performance deteriorated and fell off in quality.

Dick would frequently exclaim after competition, "I know I am good, but I do not know how to overcome this hidden barrier that I feel." He seemed to fear the final rounds, and his fear reduced his accuracy.

His I.Q. was high, exceeding the average of his teammates to a considerable degree. His intelligence was reflected in the manner in which he approached his training. He read in physiology and in psychology in order to better understand himself, and to contribute to his own performance efficiency. He would carefully practice under all conditions, and he knew perfectly the physics of the flight of the arrow and of the manner in which trajectory and initial velocities contributed to accuracy. He was referred to by those who knew him as "the scientist of archery." Although the term was sometimes used in a kidding manner to his face, he was respected by his teammates. They also would tell him that even though he was a scholar of his event, he would "never be the world record holder."

His frustration tolerance was slightly under average, but he could tolerate losing reasonably well under most conditions. His frustration tolerance seemed to lessen, however, as he approached the final rounds in each competition. He would start this last round, he reported, in a quiet state, but before the end of the round his anxieties and tensions would swell to alarming proportions. Furthermore, these tensions would result in rigid behavior and would tend to block the accurate performance required.

He evidenced needs of dominance and also at times he evidenced controlled aggression. He dominated his family and exerted a great deal of control over his children's actions. He would join his teammates in their joking about his being "the scientist of archery," but he would quickly turn serious and tell them that he would "show them" how important this could be in his next competition.

Dick's behavior during competition was often hostile. He would speak to no one during competition and would often curse under his breath between rounds and when the scores were being totaled.

His moral character was high and he held up high standards for those around him to follow. He considered himself a man of principle. He was conscientious in his sports training and in his life. He was thorough when he approached a subject, whether it was the ballistics of flight or the engineering of a building. He was more realistic than philosophical. He lived in a world of facts rather than metaphysics. He would describe the world and the problems in it in numbers, and would usually terminate discussion of a topic if it regressed into a more philosophical vein.

He was punctual when beginning a workout. His teammates said they could set their watches by his comings and goings around the training areas. If he was in charge of a meeting, it was well known that he would wait not more than two minutes after the starting time before calling it to order.

Dick would sometimes evidence mild paranoid tendencies, and at times would tend to be tyrannical with those around him. He would be suspicious of new people he met, and would frequently speculate about what they might want from him or could do to him. If a friend said anything mildly critical of him, he would characteristically terminate the friendship. On these occasions he would confront his friend with what had been said, and would conclude with the statement, "I don't like what you have said, and would not like to be in your company in the future."

He was at times anxious and at times depressive. This was particularly noticeable when his performance would not meet his expectations. He demanded a great deal of himself, and when he evaluated himself as not meeting the goals he set for himself, he would become distraught.

He was often pretentious. He would quickly fire subordinates in his building company if they did not perform well. He was conscious of the status that his performance brought him within a narrow circle of followers of the sport, and would at times brag of his exploits to them.

His decisions were often not conservative ones. He thought little of breaking friendships. In training he would frequently change the methods he employed, and this was possible because he trained himself, paying little heed to his coaches, as he stated "I know more about archery than my coaches."

Dick never seemed content with his performance, and on personality tests similarly evidenced a high level of self-criticism. This trait coincided with his high need for achievement.

He was generally low in sociability, but his scores on this quality were reasonably close to the norms. His conduct in competition, as well as with his teammates after and before competition, reflected this. His social life with his family took place within a small circle of friends. He would state, for example, that "Life is hard and sentiment has little place in it." On other occasions, he would say that "Everyone should get what he can for himself, regardless of the friends he loses." He would not sympathize with a teammate when he failed to do well. When one of his sons incurred a slight injury to his leg, he stated, "That is the way life is. It is a hard one." He loved his boys, however, and his boys loved him.

His tension level was usually high. He was at times explosive. Physiologically, however, he was very stable under stress and evidenced high cardiovascular efficiencies in the tests in which he participated.

Psychological Preparation

Dick's readings in psychology and in other behavioral sciences had led him to practice yoga for a short time in order to deal with his tensions and to lower the performance barrier he experienced in the final round of competition. However, after a period of time this approach became unacceptable to him because it was not "scientific" enough. The initial contact between the athlete and the psychologist occurred about one year before an international competition. During these discussions it was decided that some kind of "model training" might prove helpful in aiding him to overcome the performance block he had experienced.

Three types of psychological preparations were applied to Dick's training regime during this time. In the first approach, after a period of shooting, it was pointed out to him that he was now starting his last round. But because of the athlete's level of intelligence and sophistication, this approach did not prove very useful.

The second approach, just prior to the final round of shooting in training, was to attempt to alleviate some of the tension that Dick experienced by vigorous running and other exercises. Although this seemed to aid him to some degree during training, it did not prove to be a very practical approach because of the short period of time permitted between rounds in actual competition and because of the fact that the rules required his attendance during the competition.

Due to his high level of self-control and concentration, Dick found it possible to administer to himself the relaxation training previously described. In fact the psychologist merely described the method to him on one occasion, and within a month he was able to engage in it effectively without help. And because of his need for a scientific basis for everything he did, special modifications were introduced into the relaxation training in which he engaged. After electrodes had been properly placed on his body and meters for evaluating blood pressure were placed, he was permitted to observe the "print outs" of these physiological signs of activation as he talked himself through "Autogenne training." Thus as he induced relaxation he would observe a reduction in heart rate, in blood pressure, and in other physiological indices which were displayed for him.

While it was found that this approach worked quite well in the laboratory and under conditions removed from the competition, it was discovered subsequently that the athlete could not induce this same kind of tension-activation reduction during actual competition. Thus while he found it useful in relaxing under normal life conditions, he found little transfer to his athletic endeavors. He said at one point that this training helped him before competition, but that when he began competition and until just prior to the last round, it was of little help. After three months of this type of work with the team psychologist, the athlete discontinued this type of "Autogenne training" in the laboratory that included the self-inspection of his physiological processes, but he did continue to employ the method at home when he felt that he needed it—when he was tense, tired, and when his private or professional life became stressful.

For a period of about ten months no contact occurred between the athlete and the psychologist. One month prior to an important international competition, however, Dick approached the psychologist and requested advice as to whether he should continue to take relaxants prescribed by his psychiatrist, which seemed to help him, or whether these relaxants should be discontinued just prior to competition. He felt that his performance was higher after he had been relaxed chemically through these means. The relaxant he had been using was one usually used to calm psychiatric patients and was not considered a strong or dangerous drug.

Dick further stated that while he hesitated for a time before taking this relaxant, he believed it a better way to relax than the method employed by some of his teammates—namely, alcohol. He was not a drinker, he emphasized, and thus found the use of the drug a more acceptable way to combat his tensions.

As the drug was mild, the psychologist advised its continued use. He concluded that the drug, while containing ingredients which would indeed lower tension, probably was more useful as a placebo with which to combat excess activation on the athlete's part.

Following a consultation with other physicians who were familiar with the archer, it was decided that the necessary therapeutic approach was to utilize a psychotherapy in which various kinds of placebos would be suggested.

Thus for a period of fourteen days prior to competition Dick was given a pill to take each day that purportedly aided in the reduction of tension and in the improvement of performance. These new pills were described as composed of "secret and useful formulae derived by scientists from other countries." Furthermore, the athlete was informed that they would be extremely useful, unlike the former pills he had used, which were depicted as either too mild or ineffective. It was further stated that the pills were available only to him. These new pills were enclosed in a large gelatin capsule unlike the old pills he had used, which were plain and smaller.

In reality the administration of relaxants was alternated by "sugar pills" for two weeks prior to a selection competition that in turn preceded the international competition by one week. During the first day, two weeks prior to the selection, Dick visited the psychologist and was given a stronger relaxant than he had been taking, and this resulted in an immediate improvement in his performance that day. The next two days the placebo was administered. This schedule of two days of sugar pills interpolated by one day in which a relaxant was given continued until the time of the selection competition. On this stressful day Dick performed in a superior manner and posted one of his best lifetime scores.

During the following week, just prior to the final international contest, Dick was again given the new and stronger relaxants twice, alternated with two days of placebo pills. And although he did not post a new world record, he won his event at the end of this final week.

Following competition, a conference was held with the athlete, the physician, and the psychologist, during which it was explained how the placebos had been interjected into his program. They outlined just how he was primarily influenced to relax by the placebo effect of the sugar pills, which actually contained no chemical relaxants. He thus was made to realize that he had been a "prisoner of his own suggestibility."

Dick was at first surprised. The initial shock then evolved into an intellectual self-assessment of the situation. He concluded that he would discontinue taking pills and would even prefer to terminate competition rather than continue to depend upon some kind of chemical relaxant. The scientists confronting him, on the other hand, pointed out that the lesson this should have taught him was that he was actually not in need of any kind of chemical support for his performance.

Dick accepted this advice and began to realize that in the future he would need little support from a pill. He was now aware that he was in control of his own performances, tensions, and levels of activation. The psychologist and physician counseling him further suggested that additional help might be obtained from a period of psychotherapy during which he might be given additional insight into his motivational and emotional constitution.

Case Study 4

Performance Characteristics

For a period of six years Mira, a figure skater, performed at the highest level in the world. She participated in three Olympic games, and she won gold medals in every confrontation with other athletes in both European championships and world contests.

Motivation

Mira's needs for achievement were extremely high and were reflected in the concentration and severity of the workouts she would impose on herself. Secondary motives revolved around her sense of responsibility to others who would identify with her performance, such as the athletic club, her country, and her sex.

Mira's motives were internalized to a great degree. She competed primarily against her own previous excellence and only secondarily against her opposition. She engaged in goal setting constantly, and she thought about her performances, her routines, and her individual moves constituting her routines during many of her waking hours not taken up with actual practice.

Every competition was taken seriously. Although Mira was aware of her own ability, she would prepare for every contest with vigor and she would always respect her opponents. She was totally dedicated to her sport and was willing to make any and all sacrifices in order to maintain her excellence and superiority over her opponents.

Secondary motives revolved around Mira's family and her personal life. She was able to supply to her family the status they generally lacked and was able to afford small gifts as a result of her athletic endeavors and success.

Personality Traits

Personality trait tests revealed that Mira was introverted. Although she acknowledged others, she would generally not speak unless she was spoken to. Her problems were her own, and she did not discuss her personal life with others. Thus her international popularity would cause her problems; on the one hand, she would have liked to have extended herself toward people who idolized her, whereas on the other hand, her natural reserve and shyness prevented her from doing so. So she adopted a façade of reserved friendliness that generally served her when she was in public. And her "fans" were usually sensitive enough to understand that her coolness was not indicative of arrogance.

Mira was aggressive. She was much happier when the competition was difficult, so she could find an outlet for her aggression in the controlled way permitted in the sport. Her aggression at times would manifest itself in criticism, both of her opponents and of herself. She would verbalize these criticisms of others who were on her team and on other national teams, but these criticisms would appear in the form of polite and constructive comments rather than in statements that might offend or prove disruptive to her opponents.

Mira's frustration tolerance was generally low. She appeared to be particularly concerned with the possibility of a lack of personal success in her chosen sport. Generally, failure to win was accompanied by evidence of intra-punitive aggression. On these occasions she would make statements on the order of having to perform better, rather than react against officials or against other conditions accompanying the competition in which she had just participated.

Mira's aesthetic sensibility was high, as was evidenced in the manner in which she approached the construction of her competitive routines and in her interest in music and poetry. She attempted to write poetry with some success, but she declined to show her efforts to others.

Mira had high needs for dominance; she was tough-minded, and this was generally applied to herself and to her training. On one occasion she was goaded by one of her foreign opponents with statements suggesting that she would take second place. She remarked that winning was difficult and that the future alone would tell the winner. However, she redoubled her training efforts, which resulted in ultimate victory over her adversary.

Even when Mira was playing recreational games that were unrelated to her sport, she attempted to win. When she was tested in the laboratory in various psychomotor tests, she would also strive very hard to have the best reaction time, to evidence the greatest amount of steadiness, and to post the best scores in various coordination tasks.

Mira was intelligent, with an I.Q. of about 125. Her intellect was applied to her training and sport in several ways. She would attempt to devise individual strategic theories that would eventually result in winning. She was well aware of her own personality trait structure and her motive system. She stated, when the team psychologist attempted to instruct her in various methods that would adjust her pre-competitive tensions, that she knew all of the techniques, that she did them whenever she needed them before competition, and that she did them between routines when she felt either too tense or too calm.

She would pay careful attention to those whom she considered her intellectual equals and who seemed to know something she could utilize in her training and competition. In addition, she would seek knowledge from others about subjects that were not connected with athletics. She would engage astronomers, engineers, and others in conversation whenever she was able to do so during her international sojourns. She admired all people in all fields, provided they were experts and knew their jobs perfectly.

Mira's scores were high in areas that reflected psychological endurance and character. If, for example, a routine was not well executed, it would characteristically be practiced many times again. She would not be content to leave the practice area until its execution was perfected, and she would pursue this continued practice without the presence of a coach. Similarly, her opinions on various subjects would not fluctuate from day to day, and when they did fluctuate, she always was able to describe concrete evidence that prompted her to change her mind. And when she was given a personality test, she paid careful attention to every question. The time she took to complete one questionnaire was approximately one third longer than was taken by other female respondents.

Mira's sensitivity to others was also reflected in the manner in which she showed interest in girls who were beginning in gymnastics. She would applaud when they did well and offer them encouragement. Her anxiety level was high, as measured on Taylor's scale; but though her anxieties were well under control, she admitted to experiencing high levels of pre-start anxiety. She would say to herself that she would do her best by feeling afraid, isolated, and weak.

Psychological Preparation

During the time in which various personality and psychomotor tests were administered, Mira evidenced a high degree of interest in their intent and in their results. She was inquisitive about the theoretical backgrounds of these various tests and she asked questions after their administration, particularly about the meaning of each factor on the various personality scales.

As a result of this kind of conference and of her interest in the over-all physiological testing program to which she had been exposed, she formed a respect for the scientists who had been attached to the national team of which she was a member.

It was ascertained, following conferences with Mira's coach, that a useful method in reducing her pre-start tensions would be to have individuals whom she considered experts encourage her gently and comment favorably about her performances in training. This was carried out, and several scientists connected with the team would arrange subtly to be present to offer her encouragement. The coach felt that this type of ego support would be more effective when it was administered from others, as his own relationship with her had been carried out over a period of time and involved specific mechanics rather than general impressions.

After Mira experienced a minor setback in international competition, the psychologist, being aware of the aggression within her personality trait structure, suggested that she actively attack the problem of winning by devising new and more difficult routines composed of more difficult tricks than her opponents could master. The music that accompanied her performance was changed from sensitive melodies from her homeland to more dynamic compositions to instill a more aggressive picture of herself.

After one exposure to relaxation techniques, Mira became an able student, but she remarked that she had employed similar means herself in past years when she believed herself to be too activated for optimum performance. Thus she was politely rejecting formal training of the type extended by the psychologist, for she preferred to control herself in the way to which she had been accustomed during the past years.

Mira's concentration level was so deep prior to, and during, competition that she seemed to be in a trancelike state, almost as though she had been successful in hypnotizing herself. She informed the psychologist that she was not concerned with her possible success or lack of it, but that she dwelt on her technique. She further told him that if she were to think about either losing or winning, her chances to achieve ultimate success could be impaired.

Mira thus proved to be a superior athlete who had a good knowledge of herself and who could exercise an extreme degree of self-control even under the most stressing conditions. She refused to take relaxants and other medications that could ease her pre-task tensions. She was aware of her own psychological weaknesses and strengths and, while interested in the psychological measures obtained and the extra knowledge given her about herself, she preferred to work out her problems without help. She stated that if she felt she needed the help of the psychologist, she would probably not perform well, and thus would probably not win. She felt that she would have to first win over herself before she could win over others.

Thus it is believed that this case study illustrates the manner in which a sports psychologist should, at times, withdraw from an athlete's side. To have continued to work with this type of self-assured individual would have probably been indicative of a need on the part of the psychologist to somehow share in the fruits of victory, rather than because of any sincere desire to serve the competitor.

Case Study 5

Performance Characteristics

Tom was a superior basketball player, a player of national and international repute. It was apparent to many that he would become a member of the team to compete in the forthcoming Olympics.

Tom's role on the team was that of playmaker. He was an excellent ball handler, he was the team leader, and he could shoot well when called upon to do so.

Motivation

He had the ambition to do well in athletics. He wanted to be a member of the national team and spoke about it often. He coveted the role of team leader, accepted it as an honor, and tried hard to do his best as the team thinker. He was looking forward to taking part in the Olympics.

Personality Characteristics

Tom was outgoing and extroverted. He could meet and talk to people at all levels with ease. He was sociable in all settings.

His every movement was indicative of his need for movement. He was aggressive, at times excitable, and often impulsive in his behavior. He protected his role of leader with care, and would react against individuals who seemed to want to wrest his superior team status from him.

He was insistent that the team adopt his strategies and could become aggressive if someone else made a suggestion as to how to proceed. He would clash with the coach at times, as he perceived himself as the number-one director of the team. The coach in turn would be submissive, would accept him, and would give in to his suggestions and demands.

Tom was self-centered, usually thinking about his own needs for dominance while outwardly appearing to care for the team, its strategies, and its successes. His frustration tolerance was low and he would evidence extra-punitive aggression. For example, on one occasion he struck a referee when a foul was called against him at a critical point in an important game. Even after being ejected from the game on this occasion, he continued to threaten the referee with bodily harm.

Although he was a good conversationalist, generally the topic centered upon himself and his exploits. He would quickly lose interest if the topic veered too far from basketball and particularly his role in the game.

At times Tom was suspicious and jealous of others' successes in his chosen sport. He was sensitive to criticism from the coach, and after a game would characteristically criticize the play of others on the team, the coach, and the referee if the contest had not been a successful one for him.

His I.Q. was high (122). He studied philosophy and art. His interest in art was primarily as an art critic. He used his intelligence to dominate the other team members, and would be instrumental in planning team strategy when meeting another team. Prior to a game he would often "scout" an opponent and would bring back a detailed report on the strengths and weaknesses of the other team.

He would often voice radical opinions about members of the team. He would fluctuate in his feelings about others, and one day would be supportive of another player, while the next day he would often change his mind and voice a dislike for another team member, particularly if the individual had challenged him for a leadership role.

Tom was often anxious about his health and physical condition. He would magnify slight injuries and would make frequent trips to the team doctor for the treatment of minor aches and pains.

Psychological Problems

Tom had an unreasonable and unhealthy fear of water, of swimming, and of drowning. He came one day to the team psychologist and poured out his problem. He stated that "Whenever I come to a bridge over a river, I feel I am about to jump in and drown. I have never learned to swim, and find all the excuses I can never to get into the water, even though my girl likes aquatic activities."

He was careful to hide these feelings from his girl and from his teammates. He would find physical excuses to avoid the water when he was invited to swimming parties in the heat of the summer.

He explained that his fear stemmed from the fact that when he was nine years old, his seven-year-old sister had drowned. He had witnessed the drowning, and from that point in his life his parents had further instilled fear by preventing him from learning to swim and from having opportunities to experience recreational swimming.

The psychologist suggested to him after extensive interviews that perhaps basketball had been a type of compensatory behavior he had adopted to make up for his lack of ability to swim, and might even be a key to his hostile behavior. When presented with this explanation, the basketball player agreed that it might be a correct one.

It was further suggested that perhaps Tom's hostility toward others and his dominating attitude had been formed because of his feelings of inferiority about his swimming ability. He confessed that at times he would lie about his swimming ability and would refuse to admit this kind of weakness to others. He felt that admission of this weakness might have lowered his status on the basketball team to the point where he might even lose his position as a player.

This kind of feeling had apparently evolved into a marked neurotic phobia concerning the water. This seemed to be blown out of proportion during recent years when he had fallen in love with a girl who liked to swim. He began to feel that his inability to take part in water sports with her would result in his losing her affection. Thus his fear and hate of the water would coalesce into the feeling that he must destroy himself in the water, a feeling of imminent suicide.

Psychotherapy

The initial suggestion offered to him, to admit to those around him that he could not swim, was refused by him as being totally unacceptable. Thus a more indirect method was employed, which over a period of time seemed successful in reducing his neurotic fixation.

Relaxants were self-administered to reduce his feelings of fear, tension, and anxiety whenever he would dwell upon aspects of his problem. He also began to take swimming lessons in a secluded setting where he could not be observed. He was started in a shallow children's pool, and worked on a one-to-one basis with a teacher. He was started slowly, and a great deal of time was devoted to his becoming accustomed to feeling water on his eyes and face. Special water goggles were used during his initial lessons so that he would not experience discomfort when putting his head under water. Later these were discarded when they had obtained the desired effect.

After Tom found that he could keep his head under water for a period of time without drowning, his progress was rapid. Thus after a winter of hard work, Tom learned to swim.

During the time he took swimming lessons, the psychologist continued to work with Tom at the edge of the swimming area. Their discussions would consist of direct training. They would, for example, walk hand in hand over a bridge from ten to fifteen times, viewing the river, walking slowly, and conversing about basketball, his girl, and other subjects unrelated to swimming.

During the first sessions together, the psychologist would keep between Tom and the river, so that Tom felt secure. During the final interviews, the basketball player was placed nearer and nearer the river while walking along the bridge.

It was obvious that as this kind of therapy progressed, his depressions and tensions were becoming less critical. Particularly noticeable was a reduction in tension as he became able to put his head under water in his swimming lessons, and when he learned to move through the water.

Tom's joy was so great in learning the breast stroke that he began to derive a great deal of pleasure from swimming and learned other strokes. After a year or so, swimming became his second love (next to basketball). He would organize swimming parties, and in other ways evidenced his good feelings about his new-found competence. He would demonstrate his swimming skill for his friends and would even be found swimming in bad weather.

Other changes in his behavior were also becoming evident to others with whom he was in daily contact. His coaches and friends noted that his play had become less erratic, and he was less hostile and more outgoing and sociable with his friends. Unable to explain the reasons for this change, they ascribed it to the influence of his girl friend.

His need to dominate the team members became less. His need to make the national team decreased, and when he failed to make the team in the final selections, it did not disturb him greatly. He was quick to redirect his efforts and became the coach of a youth team, and derived great satisfaction from their success. When training the youth basketball teams, to help them prepare for the future, he would frequently interject swimming training.

Possibly one lesson learned from this case study may be that with the realization of the cause for this phobia, Tom had less reason to pursue his aggressiveness and need for dominance in the area of basketball, and hence his decline from a superior athlete.

CHAPTER 13

The Future of the Psychosocial Aspects
of Sports Participation and Competition

A survey of the material in the preceding chapters should give the reader an awareness of the many facets of sport psychology. It is apparent, for example, that the field may be divisible into clinical applications and into another field of study that deals with experimentation, just as psychology itself may be divided into these same two components.

Some individuals by virtue of their training and backgrounds may be better equipped to work directly with athletes, preparing them for competition and helping them to "lick their wounds" after the contest. Others may be more qualified as researchers. The latter field requires individuals who are technically capable and who can design and carry out meaningful research studies.

It is apparent that clinical applications depend upon experimental findings to a large degree, and without some base or rationale, various kinds of preparatory psychological training could dissolve into relatively meaningless "gripe sessions." It is equally true that research findings emanating from the laboratories of the few individuals who are concentrating upon the psychology of superior athletes are often less than helpful to clinicians.

That sport psychology is a fledgling field within the total field of psychology is apparent when the quality and quantity of the research studies dealing with the athlete are reviewed. Very few scholars have pursued a coherent and continuous *program* of research on this topic, and those who have seem at times to lack the technical competence needed to fully explore their data and to present it in scientifically acceptable ways. Most of the investigations reviewed are usually one-attempt studies by individuals pursuing advanced degrees, who after their initial effort fail to follow up with further research in the topic area.

The studies that are available provide data that seem to point to the validity of the following principles, which should prove to be helpful guidelines for coaches and others dealing with individuals engaged in high-level sports competition.

1. It is apparent that the personality trait patterns of high-level competitors are diverse, when considered as an undefined group. At the same time, within certain sports teams reasonable well-defined personality trait clusters are beginning to be identified. These athletic types roughly correspond to at least three of the subdivisions of the typology presented in Chapter 3.

2. Two types of data contribute to knowledge about superior athletic performance and athletes. Basic information about motor learning and motor function combines with knowledge derived from direct assessments of athletes in training and in competition.

3. It seems possible for psychologists using relaxation-activation training to initiate and to produce significant changes in various physiological indices of arousal in athletes prior to competition and during various phases of their training. At times athletes have been taught to administer these techniques to themselves.

4. Prediction of superior athletic performance by an individual athlete is best accomplished by exposing him to a battery of tests which replicate in rather exact ways some of the physical and psychological obstacles he will encounter in competition.

5. Application of psychosocial assessment techniques to groups of athletes (i.e., teams) is a helpful way to ascertain whether potentially helpful and harmful variables are present in the dynamics of the group.

6. Significant and positive adjustments in group dynamics may be accomplished after reviewing group assessments that are potentially helpful to the performance of athletic teams.

7. Certain types of decisions important to efficient performance in team sports may be assessed, using quickly presented pictures of team situations and measuring the quality of decisions athletes make about the

situation viewed. It is unclear whether this technique can be used as a training method for team sports upon review of the available information.

8. The available evidence makes it apparent that various kinds of intellectual effort on the part of athletes should help their performance. At times this intellectual preparation may be general in nature and cover material concerning the broad physiological, sociological, and psychological parameters of their total performance situation. At other times this type of ideomotor training should consist of specific practice in the strategies and techniques specific to a given sporting event or a sports skill. Mental practice between training sessions should, if applied correctly, also aid in the performance of these superior athletes.

9. It appears helpful when coaches devote attention to reproducing psychological stresses in practice that the athletes will encounter in competition. Adaptation to these stresses should result in better performance. The discussion of model training outlined in Chapter 8 contains several suggestions for the application of these kinds of training stresses.

Review of the literature makes it apparent that innumerable areas of investigation need to be explored before coherent theory building is possible. For example, sustained research programs dealing with personality changes due to participation in sport need to be undertaken. At the same time more information is needed to determine just what types of psychotherapeutical methods are most helpful with various personality types and with athletes in the many competitive sports. Further research is needed to explore the basic motor factors that contribute to successful participation in various sports. At the present time only a few factor analyses have been carried out with gross motor skills, and even fewer have been produced that deal with the factors underlying specific sports.

Although some cursory attention has been given to the matter, scant evidence is available delineating what influence sports participation has upon the personality trait structures of children and youth. Even less attention has been paid to the nature of psychological adjustments that may be important to the aging athlete when his ability to engage in high-level competition wanes.

Little is known concerning the psychosocial aspects of sports participation and competition. Although there are some indications that extremely harmonious teams may not be ones that are necessarily prone to win, there is little information available about the optimums of group tension that are likely to elicit the best group performance. At the same time the important interactions of the coach and his charges have not been accorded very much attention by researchers. A further ancillary area of study that has elicited the interest of several researchers recently concerns the "coaching personality" itself. When more is known about what needs the coach brings to the sports teams, and about his personality traits, it is believed that more effective team performances will result. Thus attention might be devoted to the "Psychology of the Coach" as well as to the "Psychology of the Superior Athlete."

Researchers have paid little attention to the psychological characteristics of women sports competitors. Of importance to women should be questions related to how participation in strenuous and competitive athletics may change personality traits . . . and conversely what types or kinds of women seek expression in athletics. As in studies of men athletes, one is confronted with the common chicken-egg-cause-effect problem when carrying out these kinds of investigations. Whether the activity attracts various personality types or whether the activity molds personality is difficult to determine unless longitudinal studies with proper controls are instituted.

It is believed that one of the primary purposes of this text will have been met if some of the ingenious ideas researched by the Europeans with their superior athletes are transmitted to Americans. The former have been concerned with superior performance for a number of years, while the latter may have the time, resources, and technical competencies with which to further explore the problem areas uncovered by their European colleagues.

It is further apparent that a fruitful field for further investigation could involve various cross-cultural comparisons of various psychological traits of athletes. The extensive use of the Cattell test makes this tool one with which such comparisons might be undertaken.

It is also true that further international cooperation will come about only if the meanings of various terms are clarified when individuals interested in the psychology of sport engage in face-to-face confrontations. The meaning of the term "sport," for example, varies from country to country; while similar inter-cultural ambiguities surround other important words such as football, athletics, will power, volition, gymnastics, sportsman, physical culture, and the like.

The authors feel that the field of study they have written about is an exciting one. Within the past several years psychologists and psychiatrists in Europe and in America have become interested in such concepts as self-realization, positive psychiatry, and self-actualization. Rather than delving into the pathology of the mind, they have begun to explore how man might heighten his level of achievement through the development of a tranquil and productive psyche. They seem to infer that to strive and to succeed in the use of one's capacities is the ultimate expression of man. It is hoped that the material in this text has illuminated how an apex in physical expression may be achieved, and how men may achieve self-realization through vigorous and accurate actions of their muscles and minds working in harmony.

Concluding Statement

by
PROFESSOR FERRUCCIO ANTONELLI
President of the International
Society of Sports Psychology

I feel that all the sport psychologists living in different parts of the world should be grateful to the authors of this book. Dr. Cratty and Dr. Vanek have here collected their impressions, their ideas, and their opinions about many theoretical and practical problems of sport psychology. They have been talking as friends on the basis of their real and wide experience and this book may be considered a record of their very useful conversation. The importance of their exchange of viewpoints is considerable, both for the well-known scientific reputation of the two researchers, and for the happy meeting between different, and sometimes opposite, sociocultural ways of living and of conceiving sports activities. This book is worth reading, studying, and meditating on by anyone engaged in sport psychology. But it is more than just a scientific book; it also conveys a noble message of human brotherhood and a warm invitation to researchers with common scientific interests to cooperate in friendship in spite of political or geographic obstacles.

Moreover, the book has historical importance; it is rich with interesting information about the first steps of scientific sport psychology in several European and non-European countries. Attempts to scientifically "psyche-up" or psyche-out the athletes, particularly the superior ones seem to be keys to achieving better performances, though many coaches are yet skeptical. But the psychological guide for athletes must not contain any dangerous empiricisms; it must have a scientific basis constituted by serious professional training in psychology, based upon the results of specific experimental research, the results of mental tests, and upon deep knowledge of the motivations which induce individuals to practice sports, to seek to win, and to exceed the limits of their own human nature.

The concept of will power, sometimes emphasized too much, is not overused by the authors. The concept of convenience (as convenient to the individual's psychological economy) is preferred. It means that laboratory tests and field tests have to be associated with direct and repeated interviews for a better knowledge of the athlete as a man. Each athlete may have many personal problems; for instance, each may feel neurotic inhibitions when trying to reach important goals (success phobia) and different motivations, and each may handle the weight of fame differently.

The sport psychologist must assume important and difficult tasks: he must establish an empathetic relationship with *each* athlete and get in touch with the unconscious and conscious problems of each; he must establish a real psychotherapeutic relationship with each member of the team and adjust his behavior to the different personalities of the athletes (he may be authoritarian, he may condescend, or he may advise, according to an individual's needs). In any case, he cannot follow common and habitual rules.

I feel it is very important to emphasize this concept because this text has the merit of being a very practical one but could be misused if some coaches believe they can consider themselves psychologists after reading only this book. These coaches, if they exist, are invited to pay heed to Chapter 12, "Case Studies," where it is made clear that the practice of scientific sport psychology demands specific and clinical preparation.

The authors of this book give us many useful suggestions about what seem to be the best psychological guides for a team, some of which are Vanek's method of model training, Machak's method, the use of autogenic training, the use of hypnosis, the use of drugs and placebos, and so on. But they conclude, and they are very right, that the best psychological guide for a team is the so-called "democratic" method, which means, in a practical way, that coaches and psychologists must respect the individual human dignity of the athletes (who are neither animals nor babies), their freedom, and their conscious and unconscious motivations.

The task of sport psychologists is not only to help athletes win, but to help them participate in sport situations in a correct way without danger to their mental health. Along these lines of thought, the best sentence that I found in this book is the following one: "It is imperative that the sport psychologist be content to assume a service role, and to be discrete in his professional dealing, rather than to be placed in a position in which he appears to be sharing in the glory of success."

It may be that tomorrow sport psychology will find scientific methods to decide what is the most suitable sport for each individual, or to predict how an athlete performs. However, contemporary sport psychologists can only try to lend psychological support to the athletes, by heeding their individual personality structures, their pre- and post-task tensions, their victories and defeats, the different reactions that they receive from the public and the press, the development of their athletic careers, and the difficult combinations of their economic, sport, and familial interests.

Such an approach will lead not only to a better development of sport, but also to a better state of mental health for those who participate.

INDEX

Allport, G. W., 10
American Physical Education Association, *The Research Quarterly*, 20, 22
Antonelli, Ferruccio, 28, 205–207
  The Psychology and Psychopathology of Sport, 11, 29
Aristotle, 7
Athletes
  anxiety of, 95–96
  clinical studies of
    Czechoslovakian athletes at Mexico City Olympics (1968), 151–54, 159–65
    Czechoslovakian "model teams" (1966–67), 155–59
    future of, 199–203
    individual cases, 167–97
  fears of, 95–96, 114
  field test assessments of, 59–77
    balance sense, 63–64
    ball sense, 61–63
    courage assessment, 71–74
    frustration reactions, 75
    ideomotor tests, 69–70
    judgment time, 67
    memory ability, 64–65
    monitoring devices used, 74–75
    obstacle courses, 59–60
    reaction time, 65, 67
    reactions to lights and moving balls, 66–67
    reaction time and movement speed combined, 65–66
    tachistoscopic tests, 68–69
    time-sense tests, 61
  hypnosis and, 123–24

  intellectual training of, 135–38
  I.Q. comparisons among different types of, 135–36
  I.Q.'s compared with non-athletes, 135
  model training of, 129–33
    coach's role, 129–33
    "independence training," 132
  motives of, 91–103
    multifactor theory of motivation, 92, 93
    novelty versus stability, 96
    secondary motives, 97
  personality assessment of, 51–57
  personality attributes of, 81–90
  personality comparisons between male and female, 83, 87
  practical guidelines for dealing with, 200–1
  pre-competition psychological preparation of, 107–28
    psychomotor tests, 110–11
    psychophysiological tests, 109–10
  social-psychological preparation of, 139–46
    intra-team social interaction, 140–46
  tension and
    competition period, 113, 125
    initial period, 113
    post-competition period, 113, 125–27
    pre-start period, 113, 115–16
    start period, 113, 116–25
  warmup sessions, 117
Autogenic training (psychotonic training), 118–22, 174

Barth, B., 11